AF228425

PSALMS
73–150

PSALMS 73–150

Rob Wynalda, Joel R. Beeke,
and Paul M. Smalley

REFORMATION HERITAGE BOOKS
Grand Rapids, Michigan

PREFACE

In Deuteronomy 17, Moses leaves final instructions concerning the future of Israel. As a prophet of God, he foretells that Israel will set a king over the nation (v. 14). This king must be an Israelite, not a foreigner (v. 15), and is forbidden to do certain things (vv. 16–17). In verse 18, Moses transitions to what the king should do. The king is commanded not to simply acquire a copy of the law (the entire book of Deuteronomy), but to handwrite his own copy of the law. The purpose was so that he would read it, fear the Lord, obey, avoid pride, not deviate, and enjoy a long reign (vv. 19–20; cf. Prov. 4:20–27).

More than three thousand years later, modern educators have discovered that students who write out notes by hand have a much higher retention rate than those who simply hear or visually read the information. Apparently, God knew this to be true for the kings of Israel also.

This series of books, known as The Bible Journal, was born from the insight found in Deuteronomy 17:18. Your Bible Journal gives you the opportunity to write out your own copy of a portion of the Holy Scriptures, just as the ancient kings of Israel were instructed to do. Writing out the words of the Bible helps a person to engage the Word of God by slowing down the process of reading the text. Writing answers to the discussion questions also helps you to thoughtfully engage the text. Furthermore, by completing a journal, you leave a legacy to pass on to future generations your insights and personal applications of the text (Deut. 6:6–9; Ps. 78:4–7).

To prepare you to meditate on this portion of the Holy Scriptures, we include an introduction to the book of the Bible to help you understand more thoroughly the Bible book you are about to write out in full. Study Questions and Devotional Reflections have been added after the blank pages set aside for copying each chapter of God's Word. The Study Questions focus on individual verses to keep you thinking about what you are writing, and the Devotional Reflections are designed to help you focus on a few of the major takeaways for your practical Christian life that each Bible chapter provides. We wish to thank Reformation Heritage Books for allowing us to use material drawn from *The Reformation Heritage KJV Study Bible* for the Bible Introduction material and for the Devotional Reflections. The Study Questions have been written by the authors of *The Bible Journal*. Thus, The Bible Journal walks you through a process of getting acquainted with a book of the Bible, copying a chapter by hand, reflecting on the meaning and application of that chapter, and then repeating the process for the next chapter. Families, friends, and small groups can work through a journal together, discussing their meditations for mutual edification as guided by the discussion questions.

The mass production of the Bible since the invention of the printing press has greatly blessed the world. However, there is also great benefit for Bible readers of all ages in following the Deuteronomy 17:18 principle and producing your own handwritten copy of the text.

May God richly bless you in writing and learning His Word through The Bible Journal (Rom. 1:16).

—Rob Wynalda, Joel R. Beeke, and Paul M. Smalley

Notes

Chapter 73

1

2

3

4

5

6

7

8

9

10

Notes

11

12

13

14

15

16

17

18

19

20

Notes

21

22

23

24

25

26

27

28

STUDY QUESTIONS

1. Verse 3: What sinful attitude had been in the author's heart?

2. Verse 5: What had he observed that provoked him to this sin?

3. Verse 9: How does he describe their mouth and tongue? What does this figure of speech mean?

4. Verse 11: What do the wicked say about God?

5. Verse 13: How did the author begin to think?

6. Verses 17–18: How did his mind change?

7. Verse 22: What had been his spiritual condition?

8. Verses 23–24: What was now his confidence?

9. Verse 25: What is his perspective and desire now? How does that answer his original problem (v. 3)?

DEVOTIONAL REFLECTIONS

The tension between faith and experience is common in Christian life. We believe that the faithful man is blessed (Ps. 1:1–3), but sometimes it appears that the opposite is true. Asaph, like many before and after him, wrestled with the problem and found the answer in the sanctuary. There the priestly work of sacrifice reminded him of the holiness of God, the doom to fall on sinners, and the grace of God to believers. There he was reminded that the life of the wicked will end in grief and their prosperity will vanish like the dream of a waking man. What will follow is divine retribution. God will show them neither love nor pity. It will be so different for believers. They enjoy the life of grace, knowing God's presence, support, and guidance, and one day they will be introduced to the life of glory to enjoy God forever. How can we use an eternal perspective to overcome doubts and questions about the goodness of God?

Notes

Chapter 74

1

2

3

4

5

6

7

8

Notes

9

10

11

12

13

14

15

16

17

18

19

20

21

22

23

STUDY QUESTIONS

1. Verse 1: What question does the psalmist bring to the Lord?

2. Verse 2: What truths does he present to the Lord to remember?

3. Verses 6–7: What have people broken down and burned (2 Kings 25:8–9)?

4. Verses 12–13: What does the psalmist remember (Ex. 14:21–28; Ezek. 29:3)?

5. Verse 16: What else does the psalmist remember about God (Gen. 1:3–5, 14)?

6. Verse 19: What does he call the people of God?

7. Verse 20: What does he ask God to regard (KJV, have respect unto)?

8. Verse 22: Whose cause is he calling God to uphold?

DEVOTIONAL REFLECTIONS

At times God gives His people over to their enemies, and the church is shattered. It seems that God has rejected them. In such times of desolation, we may still cry out to the good Shepherd who laid down His life for the sheep (John 10:14–15). We can gather courage and faith by remembering God's past acts of salvation for His people, just as Israel turned back to their salvation from Egypt when Babylon destroyed them (Ps. 74:12–15). The greatest of these acts are the death and resurrection of Christ. We can find refuge in His infinite power as the Creator (vv. 16–17). We can appeal to God's love for His glory (vv. 18, 21), His tenderness for His people ("thy turtledove," v. 19), and His commitment to keep His covenant (v. 20). How can leaning on such supports enable Christians to pray with faith? How can these truths give us the strength to wait with enduring hope for the Lord to intervene on our behalf?

Notes

1

2

3

4

5

6

7

8

9

10

STUDY QUESTIONS

1. Verse 1: Why do they give thanks to God?

2. Verses 6–7: Where does promotion come from?

3. Verse 8: What is in the Lord's hand? What does that represent (Isa. 51:17)?

DEVOTIONAL REFLECTIONS

1. This psalm celebrates the hope that at His own appointed time God, who now sustains the earth and all that is in it, will come in all the fury of His righteous wrath to judge the wicked. In that day there will be no escape, and no defense will be possible. Sinners will drink the cup of wrath down to its last drop. The Judge will take away their strength ("horns") so that they can do no more harm, and He will lift up the righteous with power and glory. While this is good news for the godly, it is a dire warning to the wicked. It admonishes them to be arrogant no longer. What will it be like for unrepentant sinners on judgment day?

2. One amazing link between this psalm and the New Testament is Christ's prayers in the garden of Gethsemane, "O my Father, if it be possible, let this cup pass from me: nevertheless not as I will, but as thou wilt…. O my Father, if this cup may not pass away from me, except I drink it, thy will be done" (Matt. 26:39, 42). The Lord Jesus took the cup of God's wrath against sinners and, in submission to His Father's will, drained it dry so that His people would never have to taste it. How does this affect your view of God's love for sinners? How does it affect your view of Christ's cross?

Notes

1

2

3

4

5

6

7

8

9

10

Notes

11

12

STUDY QUESTIONS

1. Verse 1: What is special about Judah and Israel?

2. Verse 7: What does this verse say about God and His anger?

3. Verse 9: Whom will God save?

4. Verse 12: What will God do to the princes and kings of the earth?

DEVOTIONAL REFLECTIONS

The church is at times under serious attack, but in vain do Satan and evil men seek its destruction. Greater is He who is in us than he who is in the world. God Himself is its indwelling Sovereign and Protector. In due time, He will take up its cause and arise for its help. Whatever evil may be allowed to overtake the church, it shall all be overruled to God's greater praise, and any further evil will be harnessed and rendered ineffective. Thus, in His keeping, the Lord's people are both safe and well. How does this enable believers to remain humble, quiet, and meek in affliction?

Notes

1

2

3

4

5

6

7

8

9

Notes

10

11

12

13

14

15

16

17

18

Notes

19

20

STUDY QUESTIONS

1. Verses 2–4: What was the psalmist's condition through the night?

2. Verses 7–9: What questions is he asking about God? How does this explain the psalmist's distress?

3. Verses 11–12: How does the psalmist respond to this crisis of faith?

4. Verses 15–18: What events of history are presented here?

5. Verse 20: To what does this verse compare the Lord and His people?

DEVOTIONAL REFLECTIONS

1. When stress robs us of sleep, our difficulty is doubled by physical and emotional fatigue. Yet in that situation, we may devote ourselves to prayer and meditation. It is striking that precisely when the disciples were dozing off from grief and exhaustion, Christ was fervently seeking God in prayer though His soul was burdened far worse than theirs (Mark 14:33–40). Let us follow the Master in this too: turn sleepless nights into opportunities for earnest prayer, meditation on Scripture, and intercession. What tends to rob you of sleep? How can you make spiritual use of this opportunity?

2. When it seems like God has forgotten us, it is time for us to remember His works. Biblical history is full of marvelous displays of God's power and faithfulness to redeem His people. If you are a believer, your personal history is also a rich resource for meditating on the kindnesses of God's providence and saving grace. How can a Christian make use of these things to find strength and comfort?

Notes

1

2

3

4

5

6

7

Notes

8

9

10

11

12

13

14

15

16

Notes

17

18

19

20

21

22

23

24

25

Notes

26

27

28

29

30

31

32

33

34

Notes

35

36

37

38

39

40

41

42

43

Notes

44

45

46

47

48

49

50

51

52

Notes

53

54

55

56

57

58

59

60

Notes

61

62

63

64

65

66

67

68

69

70

Notes

71

72

STUDY QUESTIONS

1. Verses 1–3: What is the purpose of this psalm?

2. Verses 4–6: What is the responsibility of each generation to their children and grandchildren?

3. Verse 7: What is the purpose of doing this with one's children and grandchildren?

4. Verses 10–11: What characterized the nation of Israel at that time?

5. Verses 12–16: What did God do for Israel in Egypt and in the wilderness?

6. Verses 17–19: How did Israel respond to God's great works?

7. Verses 21–22: Why did the Lord become angry with Israel?

8. Verses 31–32: How did Israel respond when God's wrath came against them?

9. Verses 34–36: When Israel turned to the Lord, what was still wrong with their response?

10. Verses 37–38: How did the Lord treat Israel though they were not faithful to His covenant?

11. Verse 39: What does God remember about man?

12. Verses 44–51: What plagues did the Lord send against Egypt?

13. Verse 52: What does this verse compare Israel to?

14. Verses 55–58: How did Israel act after the Lord gave them the promised land?

15. Verses 59–60: What did the Lord do because of Israel's sins?

16. Verses 61–64: What judgments fell on Israel?

17. Verse 65: What does this verse compare the Lord to? What is the point of this *anthropomorphism* (speaking of God as if He were a man)? What does it not teach?

18. Verses 70–72: What does this passage show us about David?

DEVOTIONAL REFLECTIONS

1. Biblical history teaches reliable facts about real people and events, and yet its purpose is to communicate spiritual truth and to call for a spiritual response. It is good to teach the Bible's stories to children and adults, but if we do not draw doctrine out of the story and apply it to the heart then we have not been faithful to God. He calls each generation to train future generations to hope in God and obey His commands. What implications does this have for family worship and church classes?

2. The history of Israel teaches us that God is faithful to His covenant and works powerfully to save His people. However, humanity is not faithful to God, but rebellious at heart, even when this rebellion is cloaked in the religious flattery of hypocrisy. As a result, God's wrath burns against them. God's loving solution to man's problem centers upon the household of David, giving Israel a king to shepherd them in kindness and righteousness. Yet even David's line failed, resulting in the exile among the Gentiles. This psalm thus implies that Israel's hope lies in a coming Son of David who will keep covenant with the Lord so as to gain His blessing on the people. This King must also have the ability by God's grace to change the hearts of sinners so that they repent of sin and trust in God's promises. The salvation that this King brings will be like Israel's exodus from Egypt, only it must be a spiritual exodus. How are the expectations of this psalm fulfilled in Jesus Christ and His Spirit?

Notes

1

2

3

4

5

6

7

8

Notes

9

10

11

12

13

STUDY QUESTIONS

1. Verses 1–4: What horrible situation prompted the writing of this psalm?

2. Verse 6: What does the psalmist ask the Lord to do to the Gentiles who slaughter His people?

3. Verse 9: For what reason does God save His people?

4. Verse 12: How will God show His just retribution against those who insult Him?

DEVOTIONAL REFLECTIONS

Great damage, disgrace, and distress can come upon God's church (Rev. 13:15; 17:6). Sometimes God gives the wicked victory over the professing church because of its sins. In such times of disaster, we must give ourselves to prayer for His compassion and forgiveness. Even when the Lord is disciplining His people, we may appeal to His justice to punish the wicked oppressors if they will not repent (Rev. 6:9–11). Christ is ever the shepherd of His sheep (Ps. 79:13), and He will never abandon them. When God rescues His church from troubles, or if we do not live in a time of severe persecution, we should give public thanks and praise to the Lord for the peace we enjoy. How do the church's present circumstances call it to prayer and praise?

Notes

Chapter 80

1

2

3

4

5

6

7

8

Notes

9

10

11

12

13

14

15

16

17

Notes

18

19

STUDY QUESTIONS

1. Verse 1: How does the psalmist describe the Lord?

2. Verse 5: How has the Lord been treating His people?

3. Verses 8–9: What metaphor is used here? What does it mean (Isa. 5:7)?

4. Verses 12–13: What metaphors appear here? What do they mean?

5. Verse 14: What does the psalmist ask God to do?

6. Verse 17: On whom does the psalmist ask God to send His power ("hand")?

DEVOTIONAL REFLECTIONS

When the tears of God's people flow, believers can remind themselves that Christ is the divine Shepherd of His chosen flock, present with them as an enthroned king by the Holy Spirit. He is the Lord God of hosts, the all-powerful Commander of all creation. His face shines upon believers, indeed shines within their hearts, through the gospel (2 Cor. 4:6). They are God's vineyard, and Christ Himself is the vine whose sap gives life to all branches that abide in Him (John 15:1–8), for He has joined Himself to us by taking our human nature as the Son of Man so that we might be joined to Him by His Spirit. Therefore, when the church suffers defeat, believers should call upon Christ to revive them so that they may bear the fruit God desires. How often are you praying for the revival of Christ's church? How can this psalm help you to pray?

Notes

Chapter 81

1

2

3

4

5

6

7

8

Notes

9

10

11

12

13

14

15

16

STUDY QUESTIONS

1. Verse 1: What titles does this verse give to God?

2. Verses 5–6: What historical events are referred to here?

3. Verse 10: What invitation did the Lord give to Israel? How would you restate this for today?

4. Verses 11–12: When Israel did not listen to the Lord, what did He do?

5. Verses 13–14: What would the Lord have done if Israel had listened to Him?

DEVOTIONAL REFLECTIONS

Through the Psalms the Lord Jesus Christ teaches us to worship God according to His will. God's people must worship Him by singing with energy and joy (v. 1), exercising faith in His power and faithful love (v. 1), offering God psalms with music (vv. 2–3), following the instructions of Scripture (v. 4), remembering God's great works of salvation in Jesus Christ (vv. 5–7), listening to the preaching of the Word (v. 8), renouncing the gods of this world (v. 9), drawing near to God with expectant desire for Him to satisfy us with Christ (vv. 10, 16), and repenting of our sins (vv. 11–15). How are you following each of these directions in your public worship? How do you need to change?

Notes

1

2

3

4

5

6

7

8

STUDY QUESTIONS

1. Verses 2–4: What does God exhort these mighty ones to do?

2. Verse 5: What is their condition? What affect do they have on the world?

3. Verses 6–7: Who are these so-called gods? What will happen to them?

DEVOTIONAL REFLECTIONS

God has given men great authority in the world to rule as His representatives (Gen. 1:26–28), but with this authority comes accountability. People, especially people with power, tend to confuse themselves with God. Instead of defending the weak against the wicked, they show favoritism and overthrow the fundamental principles undergirding society. The injustice of human courts reached its pinnacle of perversity when the Jewish council condemned Christ to death, and the Gentile ruler authorized Christ's crucifixion even after finding Him innocent. Nevertheless, when justice miscarries, we may look to the Judge of all the earth to do right. The Lord reminds rulers that they are mere men, fallen and mortal in Adam. If the rulers of this earth do not follow God's principles of justice, then God will judge the judges, for He is the Owner of all nations. How does this psalm teach the officials of civil government to walk in the fear of God?

Notes

1

2

3

4

5

6

7

8

9

Notes

10

11

12

13

14

15

16

17

18

1. Verse 1: What does the psalmist plead with God *not* to do?

2. Verses 2–5: What have God's enemies planned to do?

3. Verses 9–11: What historical events are in view here (Num. 31:1–12; Judg. 4:15–24; 7:25; 8:12–21)?

4. Verse 12: What had these people hoped to do?

5. Verses 14–15: To what does the psalmist compare God's wrath?

6. Verse 18: What is the purpose or result of God's judgment on the wicked?

DEVOTIONAL REFLECTIONS

God's enemies often attack His people, and they should not be surprised if they find themselves surrounded by the wicked seeking their ruin. The comfort of the church is that God will arise to help in answer to prayer. Christians can rest assured of the final victory, because God has shown His power and will to save repeatedly through history. The wicked, however, should fear, because the Lord will fill His enemies with shame and torment them with fire. While God's judgments may seem harsh, in reality they are good and necessary, for they demonstrate to the world that the Lord alone is the sovereign King over all the earth. Judgment serves God's glory. How does this encourage believers to pray for justice? How does it admonish unbelievers to repent?

Notes

1

2

3

4

5

6

7

8

Notes

9

10

11

12

STUDY QUESTIONS

1. Verses 1–2: For what does the psalmist long? Why?

2. Verses 4–5: Who are counted to be blessed?

3. Verse 10: What comparison is made here?

4. Verse 11: To what is the Lord compared? What is the benefit of each of these things?

DEVOTIONAL REFLECTIONS

1. In the new covenant, the house of God is not a building, but the congregation of people united in Christ by the Holy Spirit (1 Cor. 3:16; Eph. 2:22; 1 Peter 2:5). There is great blessing in going up to worship in the house of God. God's Word calls us to that holy gathering (Ps. 99:9) and the Holy Spirit draws us (Ezra 1:5). There believers see God's beauty and are satisfied in Him (Ps. 63:1–2). Love for God's church and its worship of God is a sign of God's saving blessing upon a person. How much do we value the meetings of the church? How frequently do we attend them? What do we seek when we go—God or something from man?

2. No one is more zealous for God's house than Jesus Christ (John 2:17). Even as a twelve-year-old child He loved to be there (Luke 2:46–49). As an adult He was often in the temple teaching (Luke 22:53; John 10:23). He especially delights in being with His believing people, who are God's spiritual house. To them He has promised His special presence (Matt. 18:20; 28:20). The risen Lord is our great temple, and He shines like the sun with the beauty of the triune God (John 2:19–22; Rev. 21:22–23). Better is one day with the church in the presence of Christ than a thousand elsewhere. What often hinders our own attitudes from being Christlike in this matter?

Notes

1

2

3

4

5

6

7

8

9

10

Notes

11

12

13

STUDY QUESTIONS

1. Verses 2–3: What grace has the Lord shown to His people?

2. Verse 6: What does the psalmist pray for God's people?

3. Verse 9: What is the result of the salvation of those who fear the Lord?

4. Verses 10–11: What attributes of God come together here?

DEVOTIONAL REFLECTIONS

Thinking about the past ways God has dealt with us is a good way to increase our desire for God to continue to show His grace. As you meditate through this psalm, follow the logic. First, we remember the past, thinking about God's mercies, restoration, forgiveness, and peace (vv. 1–3). Then, we pray for the future that God might revive us and show His mercy or covenant loyalty (vv. 4–6). Finally, we express faith for the present by resolving to listen to the Lord's Word, hoping in His salvation and glory, and admonishing ourselves and each other to not return to the old ways of folly but to follow in the way of peace provided (vv. 7–13). How would you apply this pattern specifically to your own situation or that of your church?

Notes

1

2

3

4

5

6

7

8

9

10

Notes

11

12

13

14

15

16

17

STUDY QUESTIONS

1. Verse 4: How does David describe himself? How might that be a reason for God to hear him?

2. Verse 5: What is it about God that encourages people to call on Him?

3. Verses 8–10: What does David praise about God?

4. Verse 11: What does David ask God to do for his heart? What does that mean?

5. Verse 15: What does this verse reveal about God (Ex. 34:6)?

6. Verse 16: What else does David say about himself, besides being God's servant?

DEVOTIONAL REFLECTIONS

Biblical prayer is driven by meditation upon God. God's covenant in Christ attracts us to approach Him with humility and trust (vv. 1–2). God's goodness and forgiveness draw us to seek Him in prayer regularly despite our sinfulness (v. 5). God's greatness turns us from all other gods to seek Him alone in our need (vv. 8–10). God's love, compassion, grace, and faithfulness give us hope to call upon Him even when proud sinners work to destroy us (vv. 13–15). God's mercies to us in the past encourage us to boldly ask Him to give us signs of His goodness in the present (v. 17). What concerns do you have to take to the Lord in prayer? Which of God's attributes seen in God's covenant through Christ allow us to pray with confidence?

Notes

1

2

3

4

5

6

7

STUDY QUESTIONS

1. Verse 2: What does this say about God's love?

2. Verse 3: What promise is given to the city of God (Heb. 12:22; Rev. 21:10–11)?

3. Verses 5–6: What will the Lord count as He records His people?

DEVOTIONAL REFLECTIONS

In the new covenant, the church is God's spiritual Zion, the heavenly Jerusalem, and His living temple among people (Gal. 4:26; Heb. 12:22; 1 Peter 2:5–6; Rev. 3:12; 21:2, 10). God's promises to Israel are being fulfilled in the church through faith in His Son, whose person and work is the foundation of God's dwelling with sinners (1 Cor. 3:11; 1 Peter 2:6–7). The church of Jesus Christ is more beautiful, precious, and holy than any other institution on earth (Isa. 60–62). Its citizens are of a heavenly birth by the Holy Spirit (John 3:1–8; Gal. 4:29–31). The Lord knows each of them by name (2 Tim. 2:19). God has promised His special presence to its gatherings in a way that surpasses even private communion with God (Matt. 18:20; 28:20; Eph. 2:18–22). How precious is the meeting of the church! How does this psalm give us reasons to love the church and its public worship? What changes do you need to make in your attitudes and habits to reflect the importance of the church in God's sight?

Notes

1

2

3

4

5

6

7

8

9

Notes

10

11

12

13

14

15

16

17

18

STUDY QUESTIONS

1. Verse 1: What does Heman call God?

2. Verse 3: What is Heman's condition?

3. Verse 7: What is Heman suffering (v. 16)?

4. Verses 10–11: What is Heman's argument in these verses?

5. Verse 15: How long has Heman been suffering?

6. Verse 18: What has God done with Heman's friends?

DEVOTIONAL REFLECTIONS

1. The Lord may bring a crushing sense of His wrath upon the soul of a sinner, causing the conscience to pierce and the affections to burn with fear. If so, then the right response is to cry out to God for salvation from sin (v. 1; Acts 2:37; 16:29–30). Everyone who calls upon the name of the Lord, trusting in the risen Christ, will be saved (Rom. 10:9–13). Have you ever sensed the wrath of God against your sin? Do you trust Christ alone to save you?

2. God may withdraw a comforting sense of His fatherly love from the believer, and the Christian enters into a time of darkness and horror from the guilt of his sins. Though objectively the believer remains justified in God's sight, subjectively he may lose his sense of assurance and peace of conscience, feeling that God is against him (Ps. 38:1–8). Such seasons may be compounded by physical illness and isolation from friends. They call the Christian to patient endurance and continual prayer (88:1–2, 9, 13).

3. Though the spiritual desolation of Christians may disturb us, we should be most moved by the sufferings of the sinless Son of God, in whom this psalm is fulfilled. He experienced divine abandonment in the highest degree, though faithful to God from His youngest days (22:1, 9–10). He suffered for the sins of others and was crushed for their guilt (Isa. 53:5–6, 10). He propitiated God's wrath for sinners by bearing the curse Himself (Rom. 3:25; Gal. 3:13). As a result, though we may feel abandoned by God, the Lord will never truly forsake the believer. How can meditating on Christ's time of horrible darkness help believers to endure times of darkness themselves?

Notes

1

2

3

4

5

6

7

8

Notes

9

10

11

12

13

14

15

16

17

Notes

18

19

20

21

22

23

24

25

26

27

28

Notes

29

30

31

32

33

34

35

36

37

38

39

Notes

40

41

42

43

44

45

46

47

48

Notes

49

50

51

52

STUDY QUESTIONS

1. Verses 3–4: What has God done for David?

2. Verses 6–8: What does Ethan say about the Lord?

3. Verse 11: Why do the heavens and the earth belong to the Lord?

4. Verses 13–14: What attributes of God are celebrated here?

5. Verse 16: What will God's people rejoice in?

6. Verse 18: What is the Lord for His people?

7. Verse 20: What privileges are given to David?

8. Verse 26: What relationship does David have with the Lord?

9. Verse 27: What status does David have relative to other kings?

10. Verses 29–33: What promises are given to David's seed (offspring)?

11. Verse 34: Will God ever break His covenant with David's seed?

12. Verses 36–37: How long will this covenant endure?

13. Verses 38–39: What has the Lord done? Why is that perplexing?

14. Verses 42–44: What else has the Lord done to David's seed?

15. Verse 49: How did God's providences appear to contradict His promises? How does a situation like this make it hard to trust Him?

DEVOTIONAL REFLECTIONS

1. This psalm is a commentary on the Davidic covenant (2 Sam. 7), which marked a significant advance in God's revelation of redemption. The Lord told David that through his royal offspring, God's presence and kingdom would be established on earth forever. David's sons, beginning with Solomon, failed in one way or another. Their sins seemed to put the promise in jeopardy, bringing down God's judgment and finally destroying the kingdom of Judah. Believers in that time lived in the tension of the promise of a kingdom and the reality of desolation and foreign domination. How does this psalm teach us to pray when life's reality seems to contradict God's promises? How does it encourage both faith and honesty?

2. Though God had threatened discipline upon the line of David if they broke His law, he also guaranteed that His faithful love and reliable covenant could not be nullified. This called Israel to hope that God would raise up a righteous Son of David whose obedience to God's laws would bring the everlasting kingdom. The failure of Israel's kings reflected the fall of man in the first Adam from his blessed and royal position on earth. Therefore God's promise held out the hope of the last Adam, God's Son. All the hope of believers rests upon Him. Already His kingdom has begun in Christ's coming, death, resurrection, ascension, and pouring out of the Holy Spirit to begin worldwide missions. Yet the church still waits for His coming to reign in glory and lives under the cross of persecution. How can this psalm help us to seek His kingdom in prayer as we live in the "already but not yet"?

Notes

1

2

3

4

5

6

7

8

9

Notes

10

11

12

13

14

15

16

17

STUDY QUESTIONS

1. Verses 2, 4: What do these verses tell us about God and time?

2. Verses 5–6: What metaphors are used here of human beings? What do they teach?

3. Verses 7–9: Why is human life so brief?

4. Verse 12: What is one way to grow in wisdom?

5. Verses 14–15: What is Moses's request of God? How might that be fulfilled?

DEVOTIONAL REFLECTIONS

1. Death is not a natural event to which we should resign ourselves, but a sign of God's anger upon mankind for our sins. Though we would rather not think about it, we gain much wisdom by meditating on the brevity of life, the certainty of death, and the eternity of the God who rules both life and death. The reality of death strips away our pretenses of pride and independence and reminds us of God's absolute power over us and wrath against sin. How should these truths humble us?

2. The reality of death also moves us to find a dwelling place in God that will outlast this life. This world loses its charm when we see it as a temporary home, but God is eternal. This is the great wisdom given to us by the gospel, to trust in the Lord Jesus Christ for eternal life (2 Tim. 3:15). Pray that God would have mercy upon you for your sins, give you eternal joy and satisfaction in His love, and work in you so that your works will have lasting value.

Notes

1

2

3

4

5

6

7

8

9

Notes

10

11

12

13

14

15

16

STUDY QUESTIONS

1. Verses 1–2: What image is used of the person who trusts in the Lord? What does that image communicate?

2. Verse 4: What further images appear here? What do they communicate?

3. Verses 9–10: What is promised here? How can we understand that promise in light of the suffering of the righteous (v. 15; Gen. 50:20; Ps. 34:18–19; Rom. 8:28–29)?

4. Verses 11–12: What is the task of God's angels? How should we *not* respond to that truth (Matt. 4:5–7)?

5. Verse 14: What kind of person will the Lord save and honor?

DEVOTIONAL REFLECTIONS

1. God's people have long cherished this psalm as a promise of God's protective presence. It should not be interpreted to say that no harm can come to believers (Ps. 91:10), but rather that God will work all things to the good of those who love Him, making them more than conquerors over Satan and this evil world (Rom. 8:28, 37). God's ordinary way is to answer the prayers of Christians by sustaining them in the trouble, then rescuing them from the trouble, and ultimately giving them glory and eternal life (Ps. 91:15–16). What do the images of the first part of the psalm (vv. 1–4) teach us about trusting the Lord?

2. Satan abused this Scripture in his temptation of Christ in an attempt to get Jesus to test God in an extraordinary way by leaping from the temple so that angels could carry Him down (vv. 11–12; Luke 4:9–11). The devil omitted the words "in all thy ways," perhaps because they imply trusting in God's ordinary providence over all our life, not forcing His hand to some extraordinary show. Christ refused to test the promised angelic protection, and then angels came and cared for the ordinary needs of His weary humanity (Matt. 4:11). What lessons can we learn from Christ about how we should and should not use God's promises of protection?

Notes

1

2

3

4

5

6

7

8

9

10

Notes

11

12

13

14

15

STUDY QUESTIONS

1. Title: What is the occasion for this psalm?

2. Verses 1–2: What does this teach about praising the Lord?

3. Verses 7–8: What is the contrast between the wicked and the Lord?

4. Verses 12–13: What is promised to the righteous?

5. Verses 14–15: What is promised to the godly in their old age?

DEVOTIONAL REFLECTIONS

As the title of this psalm implies, it teaches us about how to keep the Lord's Day holy. The Sabbath is a day devoted to praising God for who He is and what He has done in the public worship of God's house. We should sing His praise morning and evening—as much as possible. Life can be brutal as we are surrounded by the wicked, but the Lord's Day offers a unique opportunity to renew our perspective by faith in the promises of God's sovereignty, judgment of the wicked, and blessing on believers. Thus the preaching of the Word is central to the day. By worshiping in God's presence, God's people flourish and grow like trees. Even into their old age they are renewed in strength and declare God's righteousness for others to hear. Truly, the Sabbath is a blessed day! How does this psalm call you to change the way you spend your Sabbaths?

Notes

Chapter 93

1

2

3

4

5

STUDY QUESTIONS

1. Verses 1–2: How is the Lord described?

2. Verses 3–4: How are the powers of evil described?

DEVOTIONAL REFLECTIONS

Unwelcome, unexpected, and unexplained things happen in our experience. There is hardly a more comforting truth for God's people than that God is the absolute Sovereign ruling His kingdom unfailingly for purposes of His glory and His people's good. The Lord God only is King, ruling in power, justice, and wisdom over the entire world (Isa. 46:10–11; Eph. 1:11). The triune God reigns through the Mediator, Jesus Christ (Pss. 2:6, 110:1–2; Matt. 28:18). As absolute monarch, God guides everything by His Son to His predetermined goal (Prov. 16:4; Rom. 11:36; Heb. 1:3). What does this teach us about how to respond to the threats of powerful people (Ps. 93:3–4)? How should this affect the way we approach His Word and worship (v. 5)?

Notes

1

2

3

4

5

6

7

8

9

10

Notes

11

12

13

14

15

16

17

18

19

20

Notes

21

22

23

STUDY QUESTIONS

1. Verses 1–2: What does the psalmist call on the Lord to do?

2. Verses 3–6: What is provoking the psalmist to pray for the Lord to act?

3. Verses 7–11: What are the wicked thinking? Why is that extremely foolish?

4. Verse 12: Who is the blessed man? What does this suggest about why God may allow the wicked to do what they do?

5. Verse 14: What promise is given to God's people?

6. Verses 17–18: How has the psalmist avoided being destroyed by this trial?

7. Verse 21: What do the wicked do with their power?

8. Verse 23: What will the Lord do to the wicked?

DEVOTIONAL REFLECTIONS

1. This is a psalm for the persecuted church. Whenever believers suffer unjustly, they can appeal to the God who occupies the seat of supreme power and jurisdiction. He is able to intervene, righting apparent wrongs, and bringing relief to His troubled people. It is solemn to reflect on the truth that God takes account of everything that happens in this world. Even now, all things are clearly seen by the eyes of the Judge before whom all will stand. This gave Christ the strength to patiently endure injustice and malicious persecution, and Christians are called to walk in His footsteps (1 Peter 2:19–23). What injustices trouble you now? How can this truth help you?

2. As God's people wait for the Lord to rescue them from their oppressors, they can find comfort in knowing that God has a purpose in this for them. First, He is blessing them through the teaching of His chastening and discipline (Ps. 94:12). Even persecutors are God's instruments to make believers holy. Second, He is bringing them into deeper communion with Himself. The sorrows of persecution drive us to drink more deeply of the secret comforts of God's Spirit (vv. 18–19). Do you know the soul-delighting comforts of Christ? If not, why not? If so, how can you grow in them?

Notes

Chapter 95

1

2

3

4

5

6

7

8

9

Notes

10

11

STUDY QUESTIONS

1. Verses 2–3: Why should we come to God with thanksgiving and praise?

2. Verses 4–5: What does this reveal about God? How does it prove the assertion of verse 3?

3. Verse 8: What warning is given here (Heb. 3:7–11)?

4. Verses 10–11: What was the consequence of Israel's sins in the wilderness?

DEVOTIONAL REFLECTIONS

1. Worship engages people to sing God's praise as the trustworthy Savior, supreme King, and only Creator of the entire universe. We hear God's voice in the reading and preaching of the Word. What do verses 1–7 teach us about our response to God's Word in true worship?

2. In the worship service, there really are only two options: either we gladly glorify God through Jesus Christ, or we harden our hearts and put Him to the test. If we refuse to believe God's Word, then even seeing miracles will not help us—Israel saw many miracles, but most of the congregation in the wilderness rebelled against God. The tragic reality is that many come to worship services only to fall under God's wrath. The only way to enter the blessing of God's rest is by faith in Christ. Therefore, do not deceive yourself, thinking you can remain neutral. Which of the two options do you find your heart taking? Flee from the wrath of God, place yourself under the care of the good Shepherd who laid down His life for the sheep, and engage your heart to worship God.

Notes

Chapter 96

1

2

3

4

5

6

7

8

9

Notes

10

11

12

13

STUDY QUESTIONS

1. Verse 3: Whom should God's people declare His glory to?

2. Verses 4–5: How does the Lord compare to the gods worshiped by the nations?

3. Verse 9: How should all the earth respond to God?

4. Verse 13: What will the Lord do when He comes?

DEVOTIONAL REFLECTIONS

1. This psalm teaches that praise and worship is God-centered, with every component of praise, whether in song, speech, conduct, or appearance, directed to His glory. Worship responds to His holiness, that is, the radiant majesty, glory, and beauty that display Him as the only true God. Therefore, worship revolves around the preaching of God's glory from the Word. How can we keep our worship centered on God?

2. Worship must be missional, that is, calling all people regardless of ethnic or cultural background to join in knowing and adoring this one God. Biblical evangelism is a call to worship God. Authentic worship fuels a longing for all nations to glorify this great God and Savior. How can we reach out to the nations through our worship?

3. Worship must be in the beauty of holiness, that is, by people clothed in Christ's perfect obedience and sanctified by the influences of the Holy Spirit to obey God's commands. In our public worship services, our resolve must be to promote His glory and to please Him, not to entertain ourselves and others. Cheapening the holiness of God and His worship does not assist evangelism but robs it of its core attraction: God Himself. How can we strive toward a worship that is beautiful in holiness?

Notes

Chapter 97

1

2

3

4

5

6

7

8

9

Notes

10

11

12

STUDY QUESTIONS

1. Verse 1: What truth is declared? How should the earth respond?

2. Verses 2–6: How do these verses describe the coming of God?

3. Verses 8–9: How will Zion respond to His coming? Why?

4. Verse 11: What does the future hold for the righteous and upright?

DEVOTIONAL REFLECTIONS

1. God is enthroned. His people should rejoice, for the world is not governed by random chance or fate. There is Someone in sovereign control; right and righteousness will prevail. Life does have purpose. Wicked men cannot overcome the Lord, evil will be judged at last, and the future lies entirely with God. If you are in the midst of adversities, remember that all things are being directed from on high, by Someone too wise to err and too good to cause needless grief. Pray for others you know who may be facing struggles at this time as well.

2. God reigns in His Son, who is the Lord (Pss. 2:6–8; 110:1–3). This psalm's graphic imagery will ultimately find fulfillment in the return of Jesus Christ in the skies to judge the world, disrupting this creation to bring in a new creation and bringing believers into everlasting joy. How could this psalm motivate Christians to turn from sin with whole-hearted hatred and love the Lord with all their hearts? Why should it move unbelievers to turn from their idols to serve the Lord alone?

Notes

Chapter 98

1

2

3

4

5

6

7

8

9

STUDY QUESTIONS

1. Verses 2–3: Whom has God revealed His salvation to?

2. Verse 4: Who should sing God's praise?

3. Verse 9: Why should all creation worship God?

DEVOTIONAL REFLECTIONS

1. Consider the marvelous things done by God. In creation, He made, by a mere word and out of nothing, the substance of the entire universe (Rom. 4:17; Heb. 11:3). In providence, He preserves, governs, and directs everything according to His will (Neh. 9:6; Isa. 46:10; Eph. 1:11). In redemption, His greatest work, He delivers at great cost to Himself those imprisoned in sin and misery (Ex. 6:6–7; Deut. 7:7–8). How do each of these great works give us reasons to praise the Lord?

2. God's great works of salvation are not meant to be celebrated by a few but to be broadcast among all nations so that all creation will be filled with His praise. What reasons does this psalm give us for evangelism and missions?

Notes

Chapter 99

1

2

3

4

5

6

7

8

Notes

9

STUDY QUESTIONS

1. Verse 1: How should people respond to God's reign?

2. Verses 3–5: What do we learn here about God's holiness?

3. Verses 6–8: What people are named here? How did the Lord treat them?

DEVOTIONAL REFLECTIONS

1. When approaching God in worship, men should tremble in awe of His infinite majesty and holiness. There is no place for casual familiarity or flippancy, for God is above us in every way. He is God and not mere man. Although He is so infinitely different from the creature, He nonetheless is approachable, to which Moses, Aaron, and Samuel bear witness. So let us rely on His forgiveness and worship with fear and also joy. Why is it no contradiction to worship God with fear and joy?

2. God gave people limited access to Him through the pillar of cloud, the priests, and the temple on "his holy hill" in Zion, yet these were but types of how the King would dwell with His people in Jesus Christ. How does God's holiness shine in His Son?

Notes

1

2

3

4

5

1. Verse 2: How should we serve the Lord?

2. Verse 3: What knowledge should motivate us to worship God?

3. Verse 5: What attributes of God are named or implied here? How should they motivate us to worship God?

DEVOTIONAL REFLECTIONS

1. Worship is a duty required of all mankind. God's works of creation all around us summon us to it (Rom. 1:19–21). God's gospel message calls the nations to glorify Him (Rev. 14:6–7). Nor is it enough for people to go through the outward acts of worship, but we must serve Him with joy and energetic praise (Ps. 100:1–2), springing from the knowledge of who He is (v. 3), and expressed in the public gathering of His church (v. 4). Why is joyless worship an insult to God? Why is ignorance a barrier to worship? Why must we worship God in the public assembly of the church instead of merely praising Him at home or on a private walk?

2. The worship of God is fueled by the knowledge of Him as the covenant Lord of His people (v. 3), the God who is eternally and faithfully good in His covenant love and loyalty (v. 5). How does the person and work of Jesus Christ reveal these things about God? How does the gospel of Christ fuel the kind of worship this psalm commands?

Notes

1

2

3

4

5

6

7

8

STUDY QUESTIONS

1. Verse 2: What does David resolve to do?

2. Verse 6: Whom will David favor and employ in his service?

3. Verse 8: What will David do in the city of God?

DEVOTIONAL REFLECTIONS

1. When we reflect upon God's perfections, we can only be profoundly grateful that He is the God He is, worthy of our sacred songs and worthy of our sanctified lives. To that end it is good for us to have resolution and purpose of heart to behave in a way that is above and beyond reproach, testifying to the power of His grace. How can we live in such a way that we avoid temptations as much as possible, avoid association with those who would lead us astray, and use whatever authority we have to oppose sin?

2. This has been called "the householder's psalm" for its resolutions to live with integrity in the home and to exercise authority righteously. As such it has application to every head of household. However, it applies yet more directly to the resolution of the king of Israel to live a righteous life and govern a righteous kingdom. It is fulfilled in the perfect purity of Jesus Christ, His kingdom, and the coming judgment. How can Christ's absolute resolve to be the righteous king of His people give believers hope and comfort? How is it a dire warning to those who continue unrepentant in sin?

Notes

Chapter 102

1

2

3

4

5

6

7

8

9

10

Notes

11

12

13

14

15

16

17

18

19

Notes

20

21

22

23

24

25

26

27

28

STUDY QUESTIONS

1. Verse 3: How does the psalmist describe his anguish?

2. Verse 4: What is his emotional state?

3. Verse 9: What metaphors does he use of his condition? What might they mean?

4. Verses 11–12: What is the contrast between this man and the Lord?

5. Verses 16–17: What will the Lord do for the suffering among His people?

6. Verse 18: How will God's acts affect future generations?

7. Verse 22: What will happen to the kingdoms of this world? What will they do?

8. Verse 25: What act of God does the psalmist remember?

9. Verses 26–27: What attribute of God is revealed here? To whom does the New Testament apply verses 25–27 (Heb. 1:10–12 in context)?

DEVOTIONAL REFLECTIONS

Trouble drives many onto the rocks of unbelief but it drives true believers into the harbor of God's presence. In the worst of times it is best to draw near to Him in prayer. Whatever happens to us in life, there should be no place for despair. In our hearts there should spring up the grace of hope, which assures us that beyond the gloomy present is a bright and glorious future. God's kingdom will fill the world and all nations will join God's worshipers. How can we know this with certainty? The hope of the Christian rests upon God's unchanging nature. He is always the same God, and therefore we know that He will do what He promised to do in Jesus Christ. Christ is the unchanging Lord, and so believers can know that He will never abandon them (Heb. 13:5, 8). How can we find contentment in Christ even as we groan?

Notes

Chapter 103

1

2

3

4

5

6

7

8

9

10

Notes

11

12

13

14

15

16

17

18

19

Notes

20

21

22

STUDY QUESTIONS

1. Verse 2: Why should we bless (praise) the Lord?

2. Verses 3–5: What are some blessings God gives us?

3. Verse 8: What is God's character?

4. Verses 10–12: What does this passage say about God's saving grace?

5. Verses 13–14: What does this reveal about God's compassion?

6. Verses 17–18: What do we learn here about God's faithful love (KJV, mercy)?

7. Verse 20: Who else should bless the Lord? What does this verse say about them?

DEVOTIONAL REFLECTIONS

1. How richly and abundantly God has blessed His people. We are prone to forget the good things He has lavished upon us and therefore we need to reflect and recall the wonderful blessings He has given. We need to engage in holy argument with ourselves to stir up our hearts to praise the Lord. What does this psalm teach us about the reasons why we should praise God?

2. The wonder and infinite glory of God's love and forgiveness shine brightly in the death of His Son. Nothing could communicate the heights of God's love for sinners more than the words, "For God so loved the world, that he gave his only begotten Son" (John 3:16). Nothing could make God's forgiveness more secure or complete than the fact that God placed all the sins of His people upon His Son and punished those sins there (Isa. 53:5–6).

Notes

1

2

3

4

5

6

7

8

9

Notes

10

11

12

13

14

15

16

17

Notes

18

19

20

21

22

23

24

25

26

Notes

27

28

29

30

31

32

33

34

35

STUDY QUESTIONS

1. Verse 1: What reasons does this verse give us to praise God?

2. Verse 4: What does this teach us about the angels?

3. Verse 5: What act of God is in view here?

4. Verses 10–12: How is God involved in caring for His creation?

5. Verses 14–15: What else does God do for the benefit of His creatures?

6. Verses 16–17: What has God provided for the birds?

7. Verses 20–22: How does God care for the lions?

8. Verse 24: What attribute of God is displayed in the created world?

9. Verses 28–30: How do we see God's sovereignty over life and death?

10. Verse 31: What is God's attitude toward His works?

11. Verse 35: What does the psalmist ask God to do with sinners?

DEVOTIONAL REFLECTIONS

This psalm describes the divine works of creation and providence. In fact, it is like a poetic version of Genesis 1. A true, biblical understanding of creation moves us to admire and adore God's attributes of power, wisdom, and love. Failure to maintain the doctrine of creation diminishes God's glory. In our thoughts, we should rise from creation to the Creator and meditate often upon Him. We shall find our meditation to be a sweet antidote to all the trouble and cares of life. We should also rejoice in the daily demonstrations of God's providential care for what He has created. Yet as great as God's creations are, the Lord is far greater. Spend time even now worshiping the triune God alone, honoring the Father, the Son, and the Holy Spirit far above even the angels.

Notes

1

2

3

4

5

6

7

8

9

10

Notes

11

12

13

14

15

16

17

18

19

20

21

Notes

22

23

24

25

26

27

28

29

30

31

32

Notes

33

34

35

36

37

38

39

40

41

42

Notes

43

44

45

STUDY QUESTIONS

1. What should we do with respect to the Lord?

2. Verses 3–4: What should we seek? What attitude should we have as we do so?

3. Verses 8–9: How long will God remember His covenant with Abraham?

4. Verse 11: What promise did the Lord give to Israel?

5. Verses 12–15: How did God protect His people?

6. Verses 17–19: What does this teach us about Joseph's trials?

7. Verses 20–22: How did the king of Egypt honor Joseph?

8. Verse 25: What was the ultimate reason the Egyptians hated God's servants?

9. Verses 27–36: What signs and wonders did the Lord work in Egypt?

10. Verse 39: How did the Lord show His presence with Israel?

11. Verses 40–41: How did God care for Israel in the wilderness?

12. Verse 42: Why did God care for Israel in the wilderness?

13. Verses 44–45: What was one reason the Lord gave Israel the promised land?

DEVOTIONAL REFLECTIONS

1. Thinking about God's mighty works in the past is a good way to fuel faith and generate praise. Biblical history is not just a list of facts and dates but a testimony to God's faithfulness, to His covenant, and to His power to keep His promises. Knowing that His Word cannot fail is a great comfort to believers in life and death and gives them ample reason to praise the Lord. How can the history of God's people encourage us to seek the Lord, His strength, and His presence?

2. God still keeps His covenant with Abraham today, for Jesus Christ is the blessed seed of Abraham (Matt. 1:1; Gal. 3:16). Those who are joined to Christ by a living faith, the spiritual offspring of Abraham, are also heirs of the promise (Rom. 4:16; Gal. 3:29). The Lord's mighty acts in judging Egypt, bringing out His people, and preserving them in the wilderness prepared the way for Christ's coming in the flesh and foreshadowed the power by which King Jesus saves His people through the gospel and ultimately in His glorious coming. How is Old Testament history a book of comfort for Christians?

Notes

1

2

3

4

5

6

7

8

Notes

9

10

11

12

13

14

15

16

17

18

Notes

19

20

21

22

23

24

25

26

27

28

Notes

29

30

31

32

33

34

35

36

37

38

Notes

39

40

41

42

43

44

45

46

Notes

47

48

1. Verse 1: What attributes of God are declared in this verse?

2. Verses 6–7: How did Israel respond to God's wonders in Egypt?

3. Verse 8: Why did God save Israel from Egypt?

4. Verses 12–14: What was Israel's first response when the Lord saved them at the Red Sea? How did they act later in the desert?

5. Verses 16–18: How did God punish Israel for their rebellion (Numbers 16)?

6. Verses 19–21: How did Israel sin against God at Mount Sinai ("Horeb")?

7. Verse 23: What did God say He would have done if Moses had not interceded?

8. Verses 24–25: How did Israel act when they were about to enter the promised land?

9. Verse 28: What else did Israel do (Num. 25:2–5)?

10. Verse 30: How did Phinehas avert God's plague?

11. Verses 32–33: How did Israel provoke Moses to sin (Num. 20:1–15)?

12. Verses 34–39: What sins did Israel commit in the land?

13. Verses 40–42: What was God's attitude toward them? How did He punish them?

14. Verses 44–46: How did the Lord regard Israel in their afflictions?

15. Verse 47: What is the psalmist's prayer? How might this be related to the history he has related in this psalm?

DEVOTIONAL REFLECTIONS

1. This psalm teaches again how important it is to remember the past as a guide for the present. The history of Israel's sins against the Lord is not an occasion to despise the Jews but to consider the corruption within us all, to go beyond external religion to real union with Christ, to recognize how easily we can fall, and to flee from lust and idolatry (1 Cor. 10:1–14). Miracles, great acts of salvation from earthly troubles, the presence of godly prophets to declare God's Word, and painful defeats from God's hand of discipline should have turned Israel back to God, but the wickedness of fallen mankind is too deep for external means to root it out. Our only hope for salvation is God's love and faithfulness to His covenant. Seeing our sinfulness reflected in the history of Israel should move us to pray, "Save us, O LORD our God" (Ps. 106:47). Then His salvation will move us to praise Him forever for His goodness and mercy. How could you use this psalm to prove that people cannot save themselves?

2. What do we need from God to avoid repeating Israel's history in our own lives? God must provide a spiritual salvation beginning with the gift of faith (v. 24), not a superficial belief that passes away (vv. 12–13), but an enduring trust that produces a lifelong practice of justice and righteousness (v. 3). Rather than forgetting God (vv. 13, 21), sinners need God to give them an experiential knowledge of Him. Furthermore, to atone for their sins God must provide them with an eternal righteousness through an intercessor greater than Moses (v. 23) or Phinehas (vv. 30–31). Jesus Christ turned aside God's wrath by receiving God's judgment upon Himself (Gal. 3:13). The Spirit of Jesus Christ works faith (1 Cor. 12:3). The only hope for the human race is Christ, the one Mediator of the triune God. Have you known God's gifts of salvation and intercession as your own? If so, you can "come boldly unto the throne of grace" (Heb. 4:16).

Notes

1

2

3

4

5

6

7

8

9

10

Notes

11

12

13

14

15

16

17

18

19

20

Notes

21

22

23

24

25

26

27

28

29

Notes

30

31

32

33

34

35

36

37

38

Notes

39

40

41

42

43

STUDY QUESTIONS

1. Verse 1: Why should we give thanks to the Lord?

2. Verses 4–5, 7, 9: What problem did these people experience? How did the Lord help them?

3. Verse 6: How does this verse compare to verses 13, 19, 28? What does that imply about the theme of this psalm?

4. Verse 8: How does this verse compare to verses 15, 21, 31? What does that imply about the theme of this psalm?

5. Verses 10–12, 14: What was the plight of these people? What did the Lord do for them?

6. Verses 17–18, 20: What trouble came upon this group? Why? How did God intervene?

7. Verses 23–27: What grave danger threatened these people?

8. Verses 29–30: What did God do in answer to their prayers?

9. Verse 32: Where should people give God praise and thanksgiving for His salvation?

10. Verses 33–34: What has God done sometimes to the wicked?

11. Verses 35–38: What has God done for some other people?

12. Verse 42: How will seeing these things affect the righteous? How will it affect iniquity (or wickedness)?

13. Verse 43: What will the wise learn by observing these things?

DEVOTIONAL REFLECTIONS

1. If we are redeemed, we should be willing and eager to say so, telling others about the Savior. Whenever God acts for our deliverance and displays His covenant love, it is that we might praise His name. We must therefore learn to never neglect this, for it is our duty and delight. Whenever God answers our prayers or saves us from the consequences of our sins, let us give Him public thanks for His amazing grace and power. However, it requires wisdom and watchfulness to observe God's goodness at work, or we will take it for granted in our self-righteousness and pass it by without a word. How can we develop an attitude of watchfulness for mercies and a quickness to praise the Lord?

2. Mercy and goodness flow to sinners through Jesus Christ. He is the only Mediator between God and sinners. He is the Redeemer who has delivered men from their fearful bondage to sin and its horrifying consequences in the wrath of God. Therefore, give thanks and praise to God *for* Christ and *through* Christ.

Notes

Chapter 108

1

2

3

4

5

6

7

8

9

Notes

10

11

12

13

STUDY QUESTIONS

1. Verses 1–5: How do these verses compare to Psalm 57:7–11?

2. Verse 4: Why does David resolve to praise God?

3. Verses 6–13: How do these verses compare to Psalm 60:5–12?

4. Verse 12: What does David seek from God? What does he say about the help of man?

DEVOTIONAL REFLECTIONS

1. Having a heart that is fixed and steadfast is important, for "a double minded man is unstable in all his ways" (James 1:8). Having our hearts focused on the Lord and being sensitive to all His faithfulness are the means of having such a fixed mind. Follow David's pattern by being quick to praise God for His goodness and to pray for His renewed help daily. What makes it hard to fix your heart on God? How can you overcome these distractions?

2. The salvation of God's beloved leads to His praises among the nations and the demonstration of His sovereignty over all peoples. This took place supremely when God conquered Satan through the death and resurrection of Jesus Christ, exalted Christ to the highest place, and initiated the mission of evangelizing the world. The success of this mission depends upon the past victory of God's Son, and the present assistance of the Holy Spirit. "Through God we shall do valiantly" (Ps. 108:13). How can the Holy Spirit's work in your life lead to God being glorified and praised?

Notes

Chapter 109

1

2

3

4

5

6

7

8

9

10

11

Notes

12

13

14

15

16

17

18

Notes

19

20

21

22

23

24

25

26

Notes

27

28

29

30

31

STUDY QUESTIONS

1. Verse 2: What parts of the body are mentioned here? What do they represent?

2. Verse 5: How have these people responded to David's goodness and love?

3. Verse 8: What judgment does David pray will fall on his enemy? How does that foreshadow events in the life of Christ (Acts 1:20)?

4. Verses 12–13: What curse does David call down on the descendants of his enemy?

5. Verses 16–19: Why is a curse without mercy appropriate for this person?

6. Verses 21–22: What reasons does David offer God to save him?

7. Verse 25: How have people regarded David as he suffers his afflictions?

8. Verses 26–27: What are other reasons for God to save David?

9. Verses 28–29: What does David ask for God to send his enemies?

DEVOTIONAL REFLECTIONS

1. This is one of the outstanding imprecatory psalms where the psalmist prays for God's direct judgment on the enemy who is hostile to the operations of God's purposes and kingdom. It is not a prayer for personal vengeance but for the advancing of God's cause through His judgment upon those who refuse to repent of sin. Pray for God to turn your enemies from their sins (Matt. 5:44), but then also pray for God to punish those who persecute the church and refuse to repent (Rev. 6:10).

2. The righteousness of this kind of prayer is confirmed by its direct application to Judas who betrayed Christ (Acts 1:20). Christ was surrounded by enemies who hated Him without cause (Matt. 26:60; John 15:18, 25). Judas's betrayal of Christ into their hands was decreed by God and foretold in Scripture (John 17:12; cf. Pss. 41:9; 55:12–14, 21; 69:4), but Christ still held him responsible and pronounced God's "woe" upon him (Matt. 26:24). God inflicted severe punishment on Judas, who died in suicidal despair and utter humiliation (Matt. 27:3–5). It should be a warning to all enemies of God's kingdom and Christ's church that God will hear the cries of His people and will judge their enemies. How can this hope release Christians from taking revenge?

Notes

1

2

3

4

5

6

7

1. Verse 1: To whom is the Lord speaking? What does He say to Him? How was this fulfilled by Christ (Acts 2:34–36; Eph. 1:20–21)?

2. Verse 4: What oath has the Lord sworn? What does this teach us about Christ (Heb. 7:20–25)?

3. Verses 5–6: What will take place on "the day of his wrath"?

DEVOTIONAL REFLECTIONS

1. Our Savior reigns. Jesus is Lord of all. He wields the scepter of His Word across the world and we are either made His subjects or we remain His enemies. Those who claim to be Christ's should be distinguished by true holiness. The power of Christ's Spirit causes His true people to willingly offer themselves to Him as living sacrifices. Those who persist in rebellion against Him will be smashed when He returns to destroy the kingdom of Satan. Are you in submission to King Jesus? Do you obey Him from the heart?

2. Not only should we yield to Christ's sovereignty, but we should submit to His priesthood. We do this by trusting in the sacrifice that He offered and by relying on His intercession that He conducts in His session at God's right hand. We have all sinned against this great King, and therefore need His priestly forgiveness and grace. Do you trust in Christ alone to save you from the guilt and punishment of your sins against God?

Notes

Chapter 111

1

2

3

4

5

6

7

8

Notes

9

10

STUDY QUESTIONS

1. Verse 2: What do the godly love to study (KJV, sought out)?

2. Verses 3–4: What does this verse reveal about God's work?

3. Verses 7–8: What else is revealed about God's works?

4. Verse 10: What does this teach about the fear of the Lord?

DEVOTIONAL REFLECTIONS

1. In worship, it is of paramount importance that our hearts be engaged, right, and true. It is also most essential that we take our places in congregations of faithful people who embrace sound doctrine. Corporate worship is God's design for His church. The Sabbath is especially well suited for us to meditate on the divine works, both of creation and of redemption. There is so much to discover in them that will fill our souls with wonder and joy. The fear of God is a grace that today is conspicuous by its absence in so much of modern worship. In church, we should not tolerate anything worldly, casual, or flippant. How can we encourage an awe of our God?

2. The themes of this psalm point to the Son of God: His glory, righteousness, mighty works, faithfulness to His covenant, and redemption of sinners. God intends for His people to think much about the work of Jesus Christ. Those who love the works of our Lord will delight to meditate on them. Therefore, Christian worship revolves around engaging our thoughts and feelings with the doctrines of the gospel. How are you privately meditating on Christ's work so as to grow in your understanding, faith, love, joy, and peace? How are you doing this in public worship?

Notes

1

2

3

4

5

6

7

8

Notes

9

10

STUDY QUESTIONS

1. Verse 1: What kind of man is blessed by God?

2. Verse 7: How does this man respond to bad news? Why?

3. Verse 10: What will happen to the wicked?

DEVOTIONAL REFLECTIONS

1. Note the contrast between "feareth the LORD" (v. 1) and "shall not be afraid" (v. 7). Everyone fears something. What we fear is what we are most conscious of and allow to dictate our attitudes and actions—whatever is biggest in our hearts and dominates our lives. The fear of God and the fear of man or things are mutually exclusive. If the consciousness of God is our predominant mindset and we factor Him into all the situations that surround us, we will know blessedness indeed. In essence this is what it is to walk by faith and not sight. How can we learn to live as those convinced that the One we cannot see with the physical eye is more real than what we see around us?

2. This psalm gives us a beautiful picture of Jesus Christ. In His human nature, the Son of God fears the Lord (Isa. 11:2; Heb. 5:7) and delights in His commandments (Ps. 40:8; John 4:34). He is gracious, compassionate, and righteous (Isa. 53:11; Luke 7:13; John 1:14). He is glad to dispense His riches to poor sinners (Rom. 10:12; 2 Cor. 8:9). Therefore, Jesus is the most blessed of men (Ps. 21:6) and exalted to the right hand of God (110:1). His blessings overflow to His spiritual family (22:30; Isa. 53:10; Gal. 3:29), and though the wicked rage they shall perish under His wrath (Ps. 2:1, 12).

Notes

1

2

3

4

5

6

7

8

9

STUDY QUESTIONS

1. Verses 2–3: How long and how often should God's name be praised?

2. Verses 4–6: How exalted is the Lord? What must he do to consider the things in heaven and on earth?

3. Verse 9: What can God do for a barren woman?

DEVOTIONAL REFLECTIONS

Exalted in majesty, God has to stoop to consider the angels and the sun, moon, and stars, yet He actually reaches down to lowly men and women to deliver them from their fallen state and place them among the princes of His people. The Son of God is infinitely glorious, equal to the Father in His deity, and yet He lowered Himself by taking on a human nature so that He could lift up poor sinners into glory and bring outsiders into the family of God. Now this is grace: love to the loveless, the unlovely, and the unlovable, to give to them inconceivable privilege and dignity. If you have experienced His grace, then you have cause to say "Hallelujah" every day. For what mercies should you bless the Lord today?

Notes

Chapter 114

1

2

3

4

5

6

7

8

STUDY QUESTIONS

1. Verses 1–2: What were God's people to Him when He brought them out of Egypt?

2. Verses 4–7: To what does the psalmist compare the earthquake caused by God's presence?

3. Verse 8: What did the Lord do? When did He do it (Ex. 17:1–7; Num. 20:1–13)?

DEVOTIONAL REFLECTIONS

1. God has power to turn obstacles into blessings for His people, even in the most unexpected ways. Egypt was the most powerful nation on earth, but it was nothing before God. Man exerts massive efforts to control the least part of the seas, rivers, and mountains, but the Creator so easily manipulates them. Rocks are dry and lifeless but God can transform them into life-giving fountains. God can turn obstacles into stepping-stones. How can this encourage us to rely upon God the next time we find ourselves in a seemingly hopeless situation?

2. The redemption of Israel from Egypt was a shadow of Christ's spiritual redemption of His chosen people of all nations from sin, Satan, and hell (Luke 1:68, 73–74; 1 Cor. 5:7). The greatest obstacles to our happiness—sin, death, and divine judgment—became the means of our salvation when sinners killed Christ and He died under the curse of God for our sins. What can we learn from this when our own spiritual condition seems hopeless? How have you turned to the Lord in trust? How have you experienced His grace that is greater than any obstacle?

Notes

Chapter 115

1

2

3

4

5

6

7

8

9

Notes

10

11

12

13

14

15

16

17

18

STUDY QUESTIONS

1. Verse 1: Who should not get glory? Who should get it? Why?

2. Verse 3: What does God do? What does this reveal about Him (Ps. 135:5–6)?

3. Verse 8: What will happen to those who make idols or trust in them?

4. Verses 9–13: What three groups of people are listed here twice? What will God do for them?

5. Verse 16: What has the Lord given to mankind?

DEVOTIONAL REFLECTIONS

1. Ironically, just as genuine believers are to be conformed to the image of the Lord, the unregenerate resemble the gods of their own making and imagination (Ps. 115:8). Sinners may look impressive outwardly (v. 4), but they have no spiritual mouths to cry out for His grace or confess His praises (vv. 5, 7), no spiritual senses to experience the beauty of God in Christ (vv. 5–6), no spiritual hands to offer Him worship (v. 7), and no spiritual feet to walk with Him in faith and obedience (v. 7). They are as spiritually dead as the wood or stone they worship (Eph. 2:1), utterly incapable of pleasing God (Ps. 14:1–3; Rom. 8:6–8; 2 Cor. 4:4). Ultimately God will also remove all their natural abilities as well, leaving them powerless and hollow as vessels for everlasting fire. Therefore flee idolatry and fervently pray for Christ to save you from its soul-killing influences.

2. The hinge upon which true worship turns is faith. Idolaters are like their idols because they trust in them (Ps. 115:8). Salvation is by faith in the Lord (vv. 9–11). This also suggests that if we trust in the Lord alone for salvation, we will become like Him (Ps. 112:4). Why would exercising trust in Christ make you more like God?

Notes

1

2

3

4

5

6

7

8

9

10

11

Notes

12

13

14

15

16

17

18

19

STUDY QUESTIONS

1. Verse 1: How does the psalmist respond to the Lord's answering his prayer?

2. Verse 5: What attributes of God are stated here?

3. Verse 8: From what did the Lord deliver him?

4. Verses 12–13: What question does he ask? What attitude does this express? What is the answer?

5. Verse 15: How does God regard the death of His saints?

6. Verse 16: What does the psalmist call himself?

DEVOTIONAL REFLECTIONS

1. Such is the blessing of salvation, in this life and in the next, that our praises and thanksgivings should never ever cease. True believers feel that it is just impossible to tell the Lord how much they appreciate His lovingkindness and tender mercies. They will need eternity to tell Him what they feel and how much they love Him. However, the greatest way they express their gratitude is by drinking deeply of the joys of His salvation and praying for yet more grace (vv. 12–13). God is glorified not by receiving (as if we could give Him anything) but by giving all (1 Chron. 29:10–16). How does that encourage us to pray great prayers?

2. No one loves the Father more than the Son (John 14:31), and no one has had a more earnest and effective prayer life than Christ (John 11:41–42; Heb. 5:7). He entered fully into the sorrows of death but was raised up and entered His heavenly rest. Today He drinks from the cup of salvation and intercedes for all His redeemed to enter into His glory. He will never fail to keep His commitments to the Father, whose will is for Christ to bring everyone given to Him by the Father to resurrection glory (John 6:37–40). How does this psalm show us the joys that belong to Jesus Christ?

Notes

Chapter 117

1

2

STUDY QUESTIONS

1. Verse 1: Who should praise the Lord?

2. Verse 2: Why should they praise the Lord?

326

DEVOTIONAL REFLECTIONS

God is not the God of the Jews only but also of the Gentiles. His love extends to the world, His covenant provides for all nations, and His redemption is effective for sinners everywhere. Christ came to draw people of all nations to worship God for His saving grace. The church must therefore be committed to world missions. Our meditations on Christ and praises to the Savior should be mingled with fervent prayers for the success of the gospel in all nations. How are you regularly praying for missions in your private or family devotions? How can you do so more?

Notes

Chapter 118

1

2

3

4

5

6

7

8

9

10

11

Notes

12

13

14

15

16

17

18

19

20

21

22

23

24

25

26

27

28

29

1. Verses 1–4: What should we say about the Lord? Why the fourfold repetition?

2. Verse 6: Why will the psalmist not fear?

3. Verses 8–9: What is better than putting confidence in man?

4. Verses 10–12: What had the nations done to the psalmist? What did he say he would do to them?

5. Verse 14: What is God to the believer (Ex. 15:2; Isa. 12:2)?

6. Verse 18: What has the Lord done to him?

7. Verse 22: What metaphor is used here? How does it point to Christ (Matt. 21:42; Acts 4:11; 1 Peter 2:4, 6–7)?

8. Verses 25–26: What does this say? How is it fulfilled in Christ (Matt. 21:9; 23:39—"save" in Hebrew is "hosanna")?

9. Verse 29: Why should we give thanks to the Lord?

DEVOTIONAL REFLECTIONS

1. One of our greatest comforts is knowing that the Lord is on our side and taking part with those who help us. There is no reason to fear anyone or anything because, with the Lord at our sides, we shall be kept both strong and safe. Paul summed it well: "If God be for us, who can be against us?" (Rom. 8:31). How can a person know that God is on his side? How can that knowledge give him hope and boldness?

2. Long before Jesus came to Jerusalem on His last Passover, God had revealed that the Christ would be rejected by the leaders of His people but would be exalted by God in an amazing way to become the foundation for the church. This calls for two responses. First, we must pray, "Hosanna," not just with our lips like the crowds on Palm Sunday, but with hearts crying out for the Lord to save us from our sins. Second, we must rejoice in Christ's coming to be the sacrifice for sins (Ps. 118:27), and His resurrection and ascension to heaven (v. 22). God's faithful love will last forever for those in union with Jesus Christ. How can you incorporate these practices and heart attitudes into your life?

Notes

1

2

3

4

5

6

7

8

9

10

11

Notes

12

13

14

15

16

17

18

19

20

21

22

Notes

23

24

25

26

27

28

29

30

31

32

Notes

33

34

35

36

37

38

39

40

41

42

Notes

43

44

45

46

47

48

49

50

51

52

53

54

Notes

55

56

57

58

59

60

61

62

63

64

65

Notes

66

67

68

69

70

71

72

73

74

Notes

75

76

77

78

79

80

81

82

83

Notes

84

85

86

87

88

89

90

91

92

93

Notes

94

95

96

97

98

99

100

101

102

103

Notes

104

105

106

107

108

109

110

111

112

Notes

113

114

115

116

117

118

119

120

121

122

Notes

123

124

125

126

127

128

129

130

131

132

Notes

133

134

135

136

137

138

139

140

141

142

Notes

143

144

145

146

147

148

149

150

151

152

Notes

153

154

155

156

157

158

159

160

161

162

Notes

163

164

165

166

167

168

169

170

171

172

173

174

Notes

175

176

STUDY QUESTIONS

1. Verses 1–2: Who are described here as having God's blessing?

2. Verse 4: How has God commanded us to keep his commandments?

3. Verse 7: What will the psalmist do when he learns God's laws?

4. Verse 11: What is one reason to hide God's Word in our hearts?

5. Verse 15: What does the psalmist resolve to do? What does that mean?

6. Verse 18: What is his prayer? What does that imply about our need?

7. Verse 21: Whom does the Lord rebuke and curse?

8. Verse 23: How does the psalmist respond when powerful people speak against him?

9. Verse 27: What does the psalmist pray for here? Why?

10. Verse 31: Why should the Lord not put him to shame?

11. Verse 32: What does the psalmist need God to do so that he will run in the way of his commandments?

12. Verse 36: What can the Lord do for a person's heart? What does this imply about our need for an inner work of grace—even as believers (Ps. 119:133; Phil. 2:13)?

13. Verse 38: How does the psalmist describe himself?

14. Verses 41–42: What reasons does the psalmist offer to God for giving him salvation?

15. Verse 46: How is the psalmist an example of boldness?

16. Verse 48: What will the psalmist do with his hands? What does this mean (Ps. 63:4)?

17. Verse 51: How have the proud viewed the psalmist? How did he respond?

18. Verse 53: How does he react to the wicked?

19. Verse 57: Why does he keep God's words?

20. Verse 60: What attitude does he have toward obedience?

21. Verse 63: Who are his friends?

22. Verse 67: What did he experience through his affliction?

23. Verse 71: What attitude does he have toward his past affliction? Why?

24. Verse 72: What value does he place on God's law? How does he describe that law?

25. Verse 75: What does he think about God in light of his affliction?

26. Verse 78: Who does he pray will be ashamed? Why?

27. Verse 81: What is his condition? What gives him hope?

28. Verse 83: What figure of speech is used here? What does it suggest?

29. Verse 85: What other figure of speech is used here? What might it mean?

30. Verse 89: What does he say about God's word?

31. Verse 92: What preserved him in his affliction?

32: Verse 94: Why should God save him?

33. Verse 97: What is his attitude toward God's law? How does he show it?

34. Verse 103: To what does he compare God's word? What does this mean?

35. Verse 105: To what else does he compare God's word? What does that mean?

36. Verse 108: What is his prayer? How would you put it in your own words?

37. Verse 112: On what has he set his heart?

38. Verse 114: What does he compare the Lord to? What does that mean?

39. Verse 115: What does he say to evildoers? Why?

40. Verse 120: How does knowing God and His Word affect him?

41. Verse 124: How does he ask God to deal with him?

42. Verse 126: Why is it time for God to act?

43. Verse 130: What can God's words do?

44. Verse 133: What is his prayer? What does this reveal about our need for God's grace?

45. Verse 136: How does people's disobedience to God's law affect him? How does it affect you?

46. Verse 140: What is one reason he loves God's law?

47. Verse 141: How do people view him? How does he respond?

48. Verse 143: How does he describe his emotions?

49. Verses 145–46: What did he cry to the Lord?

50. Verses 150–51: What kind of people are drawing near?
Who else is near?

51. Verse 153: What does he remind the Lord of? What else?

52. Verses 156–57: What two things are "great" or "many" (the same
Hebrew word) to him?

53. Verse 160: What does he say about God's laws?

54. Verse 163: What does he hate? What does he love?

55. Verse 165: What belongs to those who love God's law?

56. Verse 166: What does he hope in? What has he done? What is
the connection?

57. Verses 171–72: What does he resolve to do when God teaches
him the law?

58. Verse 173: What reason does he give for God to help him?

59. Verse 176: How does he describe himself? What is his prayer?

DEVOTIONAL REFLECTIONS

1. This psalm, as an Alphabetical Psalm, was evidently meant to be laid up in the memory and heart. God's Word is a great treasure and it is good not only to meditate on, but also to commit to memory (v. 11), so that, in a time of need, it can be readily recalled. Since in nearly every verse God is addressed, we are reminded that along with reading the Bible we need to pray. Our prayer should be that God, by His Holy Spirit, will reveal wonderful things to us, so that we derive from Scripture great and lasting profit. Although believers pass through many changes in this life, it is important to realize that God's written Word is settled and remains forever the same. To our great comfort, it is truth unchanged and unchanging. What is one verse in this psalm that especially comforts or challenges you? How can you make it a prayer?

2. The psalmist wrote of himself more than a dozen times here as "thy servant." The great Servant of the Lord is His Son (Isa. 42:1). The Lord Jesus loved God's Word (Ps. 40:6–8; Isa. 50:5; Matt. 5:17–18; John 10:35; 17:8, 17), for He is God's eternal Word (John 1:1). Just as the fullness of this psalm reflects the fullness and completeness of the Holy Scriptures, so Christ is the fullness of God in bodily form, and in Him we are complete (Col. 2:9–10). Always read the Bible with this desire and prayer: "Father, open my eyes by Thy Spirit that I might see the glories of Thy Son."

3. In all but a few of the 176 verses of this psalm, reference is made to words like law, testimonies, ways, precepts, statutes, commandments, judgments, and word. Most of these words refer directly or indirectly to God's law. Why does the psalmist have such deep respect and love for God's law? Should we have that same love for God's law today? Why or why not? How should a Christian use God's law today?

Notes

1

2

3

4

5

6

7

STUDY QUESTIONS

1. Verse 1: What is his condition when he cries to the Lord?

2. Verses 2–4: What will the Lord give to the liar?

3. Verses 6–7: How does the psalmist contrast himself to these people?

DEVOTIONAL REFLECTIONS

1. There is a sense in which all Christians live in Meshech and Kedar as the world is no friend to grace or to God. It is easy to feel out of place in a world where values are the opposite of truth. God, the gift of salvation, the hope of eternal life, and our obedience to God's laws receive mockery. But we should expect this because although we are in the world we are not of it (John 17:14). What example can we follow (Ps. 120:1–2) when we find ourselves opposed?

2. Christ came unto His own, but they did not receive Him (John 1:11). Exposed to malice and cruelty, our Lord felt isolated and rejected even among those who should have welcomed Him (Matt. 12:39; Luke 17:25; John 8:23; 15:23–25). He spoke a gospel of peace purchased by His blood (Luke 7:50; 10:5; John 14:27; 20:19–21, 26). Nevertheless, His words brought division and conflict with sinners (Matt. 10:34–38). What does this teach us to expect if we follow Him?

Notes

Chapter 121

1

2

3

4

5

6

7

8

STUDY QUESTIONS

1. Verse 2: Whom does our help come from? How is He described here?

2. Verses 3–4: What is said about the Lord? Why is that important?

3. Verses 7–8: What promise is given to the godly?

DEVOTIONAL REFLECTIONS

One of our greatest comforts is to know that God always acts as the guardian of believers, so that even in the greatest trouble they have no reason to fear. Faith assures the Christian that all will be well. God is always there for us, never asleep, always vigilant, and without fatigue. He will never fail and therefore we shall never fall. If believers in ancient times could cling to this promise, how much more should we who trust in the incarnate Lord Jesus? If God did not spare His Son but gave Him up for all His elect, then surely He is totally for them and will work all things to their good and ultimate glory in Christ (Rom. 8:28–32). When do you feel most in need of this assurance? How can you use this psalm to find peace in those times?

Notes

Chapter 122

1

2

3

4

5

6

7

8

9

STUDY QUESTIONS

1. Verse 1: Why was David glad?

2. Verse 6: What should we pray for?

3. Verse 9: Why does David seek the good of Jerusalem? How would this apply to us today (Eph. 2:21–22)?

DEVOTIONAL REFLECTIONS

1. Going to God's house is an occasion for joy. As that was true in the Old Testament economy, so should it be true today. Corporate worship in the visible and local church should be the delight of every Christian. To experience fellowship with those of like precious faith and to join in praise and worship of the Lord should be the highlight of the week as the church gathers on the Lord's Day. Love for the church should also motivate prayer for it (Ps. 122:6). Do you prepare for the Lord's Day with prayer, delight, and expectation? How can you make a habit of doing this?

2. The joy of public worship revolves around the presence of God. For Israel this was the temple and throne of David and his sons. For Christians, this is the Lord Jesus Christ, reigning through His Word and Spirit. Our joy in worship comes from exercising faith in the gospel of Jesus Christ by the power of the Holy Spirit (Rom. 15:8–13). When you engage in worship with the church, are you drawing near to the Father by faith in Christ in the power of the Spirit? How can you tell?

Notes

Chapter 123

1

2

3

4

STUDY QUESTIONS

1. Verse 2: What comparison is being made here? What does it communicate?

2. Verses 3–4: What has overwhelmed them?

DEVOTIONAL REFLECTIONS

One of the most difficult trials in the world is to face disrespect and contempt for following Christ. We inherently sense that doing right should bring honor, yet this corrupt world turns things upside down. The unfairness of it grinds against our consciences, especially when our mockers are at ease in their pride and success. The scorn of the world is one of Satan's great weapons to turn people back from godliness and to weary and embitter the faithful. What are we to do? This psalm teaches us that we must take the posture of servants before our Lord, fixing our eyes upon His sovereign grace, expecting His provision and vindication, and yet submissively waiting on His timing because He is the Master. Christ carried the cross before He entered His glory, and we must follow Him. What practical steps can we take to fix our eyes upon Jesus (Heb. 12:2) when we experience trials?

Notes

Chapter 124

1

2

3

4

5

6

7

8

STUDY QUESTIONS

1. Verses 1–2: What prevented them from being destroyed?

2. Verses 4–7: What metaphors are used here for their enemies?

3. Verse 8: Where is their help?

DEVOTIONAL REFLECTIONS

Apart from divine support, the church of Christ would quickly fall before its raging enemies. They would devour believers like ravenous lions, wipe them out like a tsunami wave, and catch them like a professional trapper in the woods. The only reason the people of God continue in this world is the almighty power of their Savior. His strength is more than sufficient. Believers can revel in the promise of Christ, "I will build my church; and the gates of hell shall not prevail against it" (Matt. 16:18), for all authority in heaven and earth belong to Him (Matt. 28:18). How does the world threaten to destroy the church today? How does it comfort you to say, "Our help is in the name of the LORD, who made heaven and earth" (Ps. 124:8)?

Notes

Chapter 125

1

2

3

4

5

STUDY QUESTIONS

1. Verses 1–2: What are those who trust in the Lord compared to? What is the Lord compared to?

2. Verse 3: What are the righteous tempted to do when the wicked oppress them?

DEVOTIONAL REFLECTIONS

Whether we need protection against an evil that we fear or provision of some good that we desire, the Lord is sufficient for all our needs. His power and righteousness surround His people like impassable mountains. He will give peace to those whose hearts trust in Him and do good. However, those who live in sin will be led away to destruction. How can this psalm help Christians when their lives are shaken by difficulties? How can it help people who are tempted to run to sin or worldly security when trouble threatens?

Notes

1

2

3

4

5

6

STUDY QUESTIONS

1. Verse 1: What is the historical setting of this psalm (Ezra 1:1–4)?

2. Verses 2–3: How did they respond to the Lord's works?

3. Verse 5: What metaphor is used here, and what does it mean?

DEVOTIONAL REFLECTIONS

Many are the tears of God's children, but God promises them that their mouths will be filled with laughter. This is gospel optimism, for Christ has taken the curse of sin and won the promised blessing (Gal. 3:13–14). Whenever the Lord has done great things for us, we should praise Him for the glory of His grace. One day all our sowing will come back in the harvest, and we will shout for joy. How can we cultivate an optimistic view of life that is based upon God and the gospel?

Notes

1

2

3

4

5

STUDY QUESTIONS

1. Verse 1: What does this teach us about our efforts?

2. Verses 3–5: What does this teach us about children?

412

DEVOTIONAL REFLECTIONS

1. This psalm calls for a balance between hard work and trusting God. Both are essential. Work without trust is self-sufficiency; trust without work is presumption. As Christians, we must recognize that nothing in life can succeed, whether business or family, without the Lord. Trusting God does not make the believer passive or inactive. On the contrary it should make him faithful, diligent, and hopeful in his calling, believing that the will to work as well as our abilities, opportunities, and successes are gifts of God. In which direction are you tempted to become unbalanced? What can you do to help keep the balance in focus?

2. If manual labor and physical procreation cannot succeed without the Lord, how much more do we need His grace to build the living house of the Lord, construct the city of God, and multiply the family of God! Apart from Christ we can do nothing (John 15:5). What reasons can you give why Christian service requires both prayer and work?

Notes

1

2

3

4

5

6

STUDY QUESTIONS

1. Verse 1: What kind of person is "blessed" (v. 4)?

2. Verse 3: What are this wife and these children compared to? What does that communicate?

3. Verses 5–6: What will the blessed person see among God's people? When will this ultimately be fulfilled?

DEVOTIONAL REFLECTIONS

Strange as it is to this unbelieving world, those who fear God are genuinely happy people. This fear of God will lead us in the right and best way, and it will bring upon us the favor and great goodness of God. In many ways, the home is where the sincerity and reality of true religion should be the most evident. In fact, the home becomes an index to how real our fear of the Lord is. Yet this psalm is not limited to domestic families. Christ never married or had physical children, yet He experienced God's blessing in the deepest way. In union with Christ, single people, childless people, and all kinds of people can enjoy deep happiness and fruitfulness in the family of God. Why does the fear of God bring blessing and make us a blessing to others?

Notes

1

2

3

4

5

6

7

8

STUDY QUESTIONS

1. Verse 3: What metaphor is used here to describe the psalmist's sufferings? What does it communicate?

2. Verse 6: What metaphor is used here for the wicked? What does it mean?

DEVOTIONAL REFLECTIONS

Suffering is the believer's lot in this world. Sometimes it cuts us deeply. Yet in the most grievous times, know that the Lord is righteous. He will release believers from the power of the wicked and cause sinners to wither and forfeit their blessings. Christ knows this: the Roman soldiers truly plowed His back with horrible wounds (Isa. 50:6; 53:5; Matt. 27:26; John 19:1). Yet in it all God was righteous, carrying out His plan for the salvation of His church, the exaltation of His Son, and the destruction of His enemies. Therefore we can trust the Lord in many afflictions. What afflictions are you or your loved ones enduring? How can this psalm help?

Notes

Chapter 130

1

2

3

4

5

6

7

8

STUDY QUESTIONS

1. Verse 3: What will happen if God counts our iniquities against us?

2. Verse 4: What does this say about God? What effect does that have on people?

3. Verses 7–8: What will the Lord do? How did He accomplish that in Christ (Eph. 1:7; Titus 2:14)?

DEVOTIONAL REFLECTIONS

1. Affliction and guilt can bring men very low indeed, but in the worst of depths sinners must not abandon themselves to despair. They should pray with great earnestness to the One who alone can rescue them. They must acknowledge that they cannot stand before God on their own merits. They must look to God as the God who forgives sin through Christ. They must rest their hope entirely in Him. What about you? Do you think you can stand before God on your own? He knows all your sins. Do you fear your sins are too great? God's salvation is abundant. Do you think your sins are too many or you have sinned too long? God will save His people from all their guilt.

2. The great means by which God saves the guilty sinner is the redemption in Christ Jesus. Christ paid the ransom to satisfy God's justice. Sinners need not suffer for their sins because Christ suffered and died in the place of sinners (1 Cor. 15:3). Faith focuses its hope and desire upon Jesus Christ. He is the only Mediator between God and men, for He gave Himself as "a ransom for all" (1 Tim. 2:5–6). Do you trust in Christ alone for salvation from sin? If so, then how has your faith evidenced itself in a childlike fear of the Lord?

Notes

1

2

3

STUDY QUESTIONS

1. Verse 1: What mindset has David taken?

2. Verse 2: What does he compare himself to

DEVOTIONAL REFLECTIONS

Pride causes great trouble, but humility brings right thinking, speaking, and living. It is a grace most pleasing to God. True humility expresses itself in confident reliance on the Lord. It releases a person from the strife of arrogance and personal ambition. It quiets the heart with contentment to live near to God. It makes us like Christ, who did not use His equality with the Father for selfish pursuits, but became a humble and crucified servant to obey His Father (Phil. 2:5–8). Yet He counted it His food to do His Father's will (John 4:34), living in joyful hope (Heb. 12:2). Why is humility so essential to peace and hope?

Notes

Chapter 132

1

2

3

4

5

6

7

8

9

10

11

Notes

12

13

14

15

16

17

18

STUDY QUESTIONS

1. Verses 1–5: What did David swear to the Lord?

2. Verse 7: What have God's people resolved to do?

3. Verse 9: How does this verse compare to verse 16?

4. Verses 11–12: What did the Lord swear to David?

5. Verses 13–14: What has the Lord chosen and desired?

6. Verse 17: What two images are used here? What do they mean
   (1 Sam. 2:10; 1 Kings 11:36)?

DEVOTIONAL REFLECTIONS

David's resolution to establish a place for God's holy presence (Ps. 132:4–5) reminds us that one great purpose of God's king is to build God's temple. Nothing is more important to the kingdom of God than worshiping the Lord. His presence with His people is their joy and His glory. Jesus Christ is the anointed Son of David and the fulfillment of these promises (Acts 2:29–30). He was born in Bethlehem Ephratah (Mic. 5:2). He declared, "I will build my church" (Matt. 16:18). Christ is Lord of heaven and earth, and in Him the presence of God is coming to all nations (Matt. 28:18–20). God's worshipers no longer gather around a physical location, but worship God through Christ in the Holy Spirit regardless of where they meet for public worship, for they are the temple of the living God (John 4:21–24; Eph. 2:18–22). How does God's covenant with David encourage us to pray, "Thy kingdom come"? How does it help us understand what we are asking for in those words?

Notes

1

2

3

1. Verses 1–2: What does David compare unity among brothers to? What does this suggest (Ex. 30:30)?

2. Verse 3: What else does David compare unity to? What does this mean (Hos. 14:5)?

DEVOTIONAL REFLECTIONS

1. Unity, based on truth, is most desirable. It is to God's glory and His people's good, and therefore we must never do anything to produce discord or division. Since the Holy Spirit is the source of love and peace, we must constantly pray to be filled with the Spirit, and the whole church needs to pray for further outpourings of the Spirit. Is this a petition in your daily prayers? Is it a petition regularly heard in your prayer meetings?

2. Just as the unity of Israel was compared to the anointing oil that flowed from Aaron's head down to his garments, so the spiritual unity of the church consists of the Holy Spirit who anointed Christ and now overflows to every member of His body (1 Cor. 12:12–13). Our unity is found not by ignoring doctrine but in knowing and trusting Jesus Christ (Eph. 4:13). He is our great High Priest, and our worship revolves around drawing near to God through Him and confessing our hope in Him (Heb. 10:19–22). How does making Christ the center of our worship promote unity in the church?

Notes

1

2

3

STUDY QUESTIONS

1. Verses 1–2: Whom does the psalmist speak to? What does he tell them to do?

2. Verse 3: What does he pray?

DEVOTIONAL REFLECTIONS

1. Very special attention should be given to public worship since man's chief end is to glorify and enjoy God. Just how much do we love God's house and how devoted are we to Sabbath worship? Tiredness can sometimes hinder us in worship, but it should never be an excuse to leave it off altogether. Godly priests saw it as their duty to worship even at night, and we do well to be as zealous and keen as they were.

2. Just as the priests led Israel's praise and declared God's blessing upon the people (Lev. 9:22; Num. 6:22–27), so the Lord Christ, our great High Priest, leads the spiritual Israel to praise God and receive His blessings (Luke 24:50; Rom. 15:8–13; Heb. 2:11–13). As the King reigning in the heavenly Zion, Christ applies God's blessing to His people. In practical terms, how can Christians bless God *through Christ* and receive God's blessing *through Christ* when they meet for worship?

Notes

1

2

3

4

5

6

7

8

9

10

Notes

11

12

13

14

15

16

17

18

19

Notes

20

21

STUDY QUESTIONS

1. Verse 3: Why should we praise the Lord?

2. Verses 5–6: What makes the Lord greater than all (so-called) gods? How does verse 6 compare to Psalm 115:3?

3. Verses 8–9: How did the Lord show His greatness in Egypt?

4. Verse 12: What did the Lord do for Israel?

5. Verse 14: How does this verse compare to Deuteronomy 32:36?

6. Verses 15–18: How do these verses compare to Psalm 115:4–8?

7. Verses 19–20: How do these verses compare to Psalm 115:9–11?

DEVOTIONAL REFLECTIONS

1. God is good and the source of all the good we enjoy. He is also great and able to do anything and everything for His people. Therefore He is most worthy of our praise. The psalmist praises God for His election, redemption, and preservation. Praise must go forth from the church to the world that men might come to know and fear the Lord, turning from their idols to the true God. It is solemn to reflect on the fact that the matter and manner of our praise are means of instructing unbelievers. Does our worship impress men with God's greatness, sovereignty, and holiness, or is it mere entertainment to soothe the worshipers?

2. The promise that God will judge His people (v. 14) is a fearful warning to those who profess faith in Jesus Christ but later turn away from Him forever (Heb. 10:29–31). They have known the true God but have chosen worthless idols, provoking God's eternal wrath. What reasons does this psalm give for why it is foolish to reject the Lord?

Notes

Chapter 136

1

2

3

4

5

6

7

8

9

10

11

Notes

12

13

14

15

16

17

18

19

20

21

22

Notes

23

24

25

26

STUDY QUESTIONS

1. Verse 1: What do you notice about every verse in this psalm?

2. Verses 2–3: What titles are given to God here?

3. Verses 5–9: What great works of God are mentioned here?

4. Verses 10–12: What did the Lord do for Israel in Egypt? How does this show His faithful love (KJV, mercy)?

5. Verses 13–15: What did the Lord do at the Red Sea?

6. Verses 17–20: What did the Lord do to the kings of nations that opposed Israel?

7. Verses 21–22: How did the Lord show His love to Israel in the promised land?

8. Verse 25: What does the Lord do for "all flesh"?

DEVOTIONAL REFLECTIONS

1. This psalm provides a pattern for praising God's faithful love. It begins by reflecting on who God is both in His goodness and greatness (vv. 1–3). The psalmist enumerates His amazing works (v. 4) of creation (vv. 5–9), redemption (vv. 10–15), and leading His people to their inheritance (vv. 16–22). It concludes by considering the gracious and compassionate nature of His love to the lowly and the breadth of His blessings (vv. 23–25). Why is it good to praise God with songs that recount His great works in history and highlight His attributes?

2. The refrain repeated in every verse implies that all God does throughout the world is soaked in His faithful love. Yet the focus of the psalm is upon the salvation of Israel, which is a type of salvation through Christ. In Him the love of God comes to its grandest expression and accomplishes its eternal purpose toward His elect people. What reasons from God's work in your own life motivate you to say to God, "Thy mercy endureth forever"?

Notes

1

2

3

4

5

6

7

8

9

1. Verse 1: Where is this psalm set? What is the situation (2 Chron. 36:15–21)?

2. Verses 5–6: What does the psalmist resolve?

3. Verse 8: What is this a desire for?

DEVOTIONAL REFLECTIONS

1. Sin brings inevitable consequences. Vengeance is the Lord's. Though the enemies of God's people may mock their sufferings, one day the Lord will bring back on the wicked what they have done. Even as believers may weep over the persecuted church, they can also rejoice that Christ is coming and will make all things right. How can this hope enable us to wait patiently and not take personal revenge?

2. When God finally deals with sinners on judgment day, it will mean far worse than anything written here, for the Lord will banish them from all enjoyment of His goodness into the everlasting fires of hell. The Lord does not take lightly the persecution of His children. If you have harmed or mocked believers in Jesus Christ, repent quickly before it is too late. Pray for others who have fallen into this sin.

1

2

3

4

5

6

7

Notes

8

1. Verse 4: Who will praise the Lord? Why is this surprising?

2. Verse 6: How does the Lord relate to the lowly and the proud?

3. Verse 8: What is David's confidence? What is his prayer?

DEVOTIONAL REFLECTIONS

1. Christians must not fear to confess Christ before the world and give praise to God in the presence of great men and women (Matt. 10:18, 26, 32–33). Though the rich, powerful, and celebrities of the world may be regarded as gods, they will die like all other men (Ps. 82:6–7). They need to hear of the glories of the only true God, so that they can be saved and give Him the praise that He deserves. Is there anyone whom you find it very hard to speak to about the Lord? Why is this? How can you overcome that fear?

2. God has chosen to invest His glory in His Word, not to make the Bible into God, but so that people will honor the Lord in the way they honor His Word. A mark of true conversion is receiving the Holy Scriptures not as the word of men, but as the powerful and authoritative Word of God (1 Thess. 2:13). How should this affect our attitude when we hear the preaching of God's Word? How should this affect the way that preachers study and proclaim the Word?

Notes

Chapter 139

1

2

3

4

5

6

7

8

9

10

11

Notes

12

13

14

15

16

17

18

19

Notes

20

21

22

23

24

STUDY QUESTIONS

1. Verses 1–3: What does this reveal about God? What do we call this attribute of God?

2. Verse 6: What does David say about God's knowledge of him (vv. 17–18)?

3. Verses 7–8: What does this tell us about God? What do we call this attribute?

4. Verses 13–14: What does this reveal about the growth of a child in the womb?

5. Verse 16: What is written in God's "book"? What does this mean (Jer. 1:5)?

6. Verses 19–20: What does David say about the wicked?

7. Verse 21: What is David's attitude toward those who hate God?

8. Verses 23–24: What was David's prayer? How would you put it in your own words?

1. This psalm is a wonderful example of the connection between theology and life. Doctrine should impact our hearts and affect the way that we live. Believing that God sees and knows everything comforts us because He therefore knows our needs and can supply them. However, this same truth challenges us, for nothing escapes His glance, not even our secret sins. Therefore we should be careful, walking in the fear of God. Here is the sum. Since God is omniscient, He knows me personally and is with me constantly. Since God is the Creator, He owns me completely. Since God is righteous, He demands my loyalty. Learn to factor God into all of life. Pick one of God's attributes mentioned in this psalm. What difference should it make in your life today?

2. Before Christ left to ascend into heaven, He sent His church to make disciples of all nations, and He promised, "I am with you always, even unto the end of the world" (Matt. 28:20). Knowing that Christ is with us, indeed that His special presence is promised to every gathering of the true church (Matt. 18:20), is a great comfort as we do His work in the world. How could that encourage people to move to other locations, even to other nations, in order to advance the kingdom of God there?

Notes

Chapter 140

1

2

3

4

5

6

7

8

Notes

9

10

11

12

13

STUDY QUESTIONS

1. Verse 1: Whom does David ask God to deliver him from?

2. Verse 3: What does David compare them to (Rom. 3:13)? What does that mean?

3. Verse 6: How does David address the Lord? Why is that a reason to hear his prayers?

4. Verse 12: What does David know about the Lord?

DEVOTIONAL REFLECTIONS

1. Given that we live in a world where Satan is very active, we should at all times be vigilant. Believers cannot do without God for a single day, for only He can keep us in the evil day when we feel particularly under attack. He alone is a sovereign Protector. It is the greatest of comforts to have God on our side, maintaining our cause. Since He does not change, nor ever will, we have confidence for the future, even for the eternal future. Instead of being cast down, we should abound in hope. Spiritual alertness and optimistic hope are key motives to a life of continual prayer. If we rarely pray for God to defend us against evil, what does that say about us?

2. The words of fallen man are full of secret poison (v. 3; Rom. 3:13). One of the earliest signs of human depravity is sinful speech (Ps. 58:3). Though many would deny it, Christ taught that our speech reveals our hearts, and God will judge our spiritual conditions in part by the patterns of our talk (Matt. 12:34–37). Examine how you talk to people, praying that God will reveal to you any pride, sexual lust, greed, sinful anger, hatred, and lying. How does the way we talk to each other show that we need Jesus Christ to save us from sin?

Notes

1

2

3

4

5

6

7

Notes

8

9

10

1. Verse 2: What does David compare his prayers to?

2. Verse 5: What was David's attitude toward receiving correction from the righteous?

3. Verse 9: What was David's request concerning the snares and traps (KJV, gins) of the wicked?

DEVOTIONAL REFLECTIONS

1. Prayer is vital and must never be neglected, particularly in difficult times. The storms of life should always drive us into the harbor of God's presence. Notice what David asked God to give him: salvation from sin, accountability from godly friends, rescue from the traps of the world, and judgment upon the wicked. How often do you pray for such things?

2. Comparing prayer to incense is most instructive and encouraging. The smoke arising from the altar would waft over the veil entering the inner sanctuary that represented the immediate presence of God. So it is that prayer is the earthly means whereby we may enter into God's presence. Prayer takes us as close to God as we can get this side of the veil in this life. The comparison of prayer to incense also reminds us that all our prayers depend upon the intercession of the High Priest, Jesus Christ. His intercessions fill the prayers of a believer with a delightful fragrance to God, for Christ obeyed God perfectly and paid for our sins completely. True prayer must always be offered to God by faith in Him. What confidence does it give you to know that Christ is interceding for you (Rom. 8:31–39)?

Notes

1

2

3

4

5

6

7

1. Verses 3–4: What was David's problem?

2. Verse 5: What was David's hope?

DEVOTIONAL REFLECTIONS

In the worst of life's troubles, God is only a prayer away from us and, if we turn to Him, He will make known to us His power and comfort. Remember, God is a present help in times of trouble. It is a relief to realize that God knows our path and feels concern and sympathy for us in this state. Furthermore, knowing exactly where and how we are, He will draw near to help. Friends may let us down, but God will never fail those who trust in Him. Christ understands exactly how it feels to be alone (Matt. 26:31, 56), and in His sympathy He helps all who come to God through Him (Heb. 4:15–16). How will hoping in God's faithfulness to His covenant promises affect the attitude of our prayers?

Notes

1

2

3

4

5

6

7

Notes

8

9

10

11

12

STUDY QUESTIONS

1. Verse 2: What will be the outcome if God judges His servants by their works?

2. Verse 5: How did David respond to this crisis? Why was that wise?

3. Verse 10: What was David's prayer?

4. Verses 11–12: What reasons does David give why God should give him life (in KJV, this phrase is quicken) and cut off his enemies?

DEVOTIONAL REFLECTIONS

We pray with hands stretched out to heaven (v. 6) and souls lifted up to God (v. 8) because we are like beggars seeking everything from Him. As human beings who fell into sin with our first father, Adam, all our prayers are ultimately prayers for Christ, to whom the Father joins sinners when He calls them to faith in Him (1 Cor. 1:23–24, 30). We need wisdom from God, and so we must set our minds upon God's Word (Ps. 143:5) with prayers for Christ to be our *wisdom*. We need justification in God's sight and cannot obtain a righteous status by our own merit (v. 2), so we must pray for Christ to be our *righteousness*. We need to become obedient to God's will, so we must pray that Christ would be our *sanctification* through the Holy Spirit (v. 10). We pray for deliverance from enemies, persecutors, and death (vv. 3, 7, 9, 12), and Christ is our *redemption*. Of which of these do you most feel in need right now? How can you seek for what you need in Christ?

Notes

1

2

3

4

5

6

7

8

9

Notes

10

11

12

13

14

15

STUDY QUESTIONS

1. Verse 1: How did the Lord strengthen David? How might we apply that today (Eph. 6:10–12)?

2. Verses 3–4: What does this teach us about mankind and God's attention to him?

3. Verse 8: How does David describe his enemies (v. 11)?

4. Verse 12: What images are used of sons and daughters? What might they mean?

5. Verse 15: Who is blessed (KJV, happy)?

DEVOTIONAL REFLECTIONS

1. Trust in the Lord goes hand in hand with a sense of how small and insignificant we are (Ps. 144:2–4). When our hearts and mouths are full of boasts about ourselves, it is hard to sing God's praises with much interest. However, when we see ourselves as sinners quickly passing from this earth to face judgment, then we will count ourselves blessed only if the Lord is our God and we are in covenant relationship with Him through faith in Jesus Christ. How can meditating on the vanity of man (v. 4) help you to trust in the Lord and give all the glory to Him?

2. David, the divinely empowered warrior (v. 1), was a shadow and type of Christ. In an amazing act of condescension, the Son of God became a mortal man (v. 4). He placed Himself in a position of complete dependence upon the Father (v. 2), who amply supplied Him with the Spirit to overcome the devil. Christ is the Servant of the Lord (v. 10). The Lord Jesus perfectly obeyed the law of God, winning the riches of glory promised to covenant keepers as Israel never could (vv. 12–15). Now His spiritual offspring inherit the blessings He deserves. Christ will tear open the skies and come down with fire and glory to destroy His enemies, save believers from their persecutors, and bring them into His blessing. Can you say with the church of Jesus Christ, "Happy is that people, whose God is the LORD" (v. 15)?

Notes

1

2

3

4

5

6

7

8

9

10

Notes

11

12

13

14

15

16

17

18

19

Notes

20

21

STUDY QUESTIONS

1. Verse 3: What does this verse teach us about God?

2. Verses 4–6: What words are used to describe God and His works?

3. Verses 8–9: What attributes of God are listed here?

4. Verses 11–13: What does this teach us about God's kingdom or reign?

5. Verses 15–16: What does this teach us about what God is doing all the time?

6. Verses 18–19: How do these verses encourage us to pray?

7. Verse 20: How does God treat those who love Him and those who are wicked?

DEVOTIONAL REFLECTIONS

1. Meditation upon God is vital to spiritual life, for as we comprehend more of God, the knowledge of Him will provide matter for more excellent praise. This psalm offers a lyrical catalog of God's attributes. In what verses do you find reference to the following attributes: greatness, incomprehensibility, power, majesty, fearsomeness, goodness, righteousness, grace, compassion, patience, faithful love, glory, kingdom, eternality, presence, and holiness? Focus on one of these. What does it mean? How has God displayed it through His works in Jesus Christ?

2. Singing praise is a means of instruction and edification. It is good for this generation to sing God's praise to the next, and therefore we should encourage little children to be present in the congregation. Let them know how His love for us draws forth our love for Him and how we have learned to look to Him for all our needs. Then shall the prayer of the ages—"Hallowed be thy name"—be answered. What opportunities do you have to pass on the joy of worship to the next generation?

Notes

1

2

3

4

5

6

7

8

9

10

STUDY QUESTIONS

1. Verses 3–4: In whom should we not put our trust? Why not?

2. Verses 5–6: In whom should we put our hope? Why?

3. Verses 7–9: To whom does the Lord give justice and relief?

DEVOTIONAL REFLECTIONS

Only believers know true happiness. The world thinks our religion is gloomy and miserable, but they could not be more mistaken. We are the happiest people. God is our God. He is the all-powerful Lord of all His creation. He is faithful to all His promises. He acts with justice and compassion for the oppressed. He loves those who walk in faith and obedience. His kingdom will never end. In every way, the Lord is the hope and joy of believers. For all His qualities belong to them and serve their good if they are joined to Jesus Christ by a living faith. As a result, their happiness is far deeper, more stable, and more satisfying than that of those who trust in man. One of the best ways for believers to enjoy their happiness and demonstrate it to the watching world is by praising the Lord. Do you have a habit of praising God? Why or why not? How can you develop a habit of praising Him as long as you live?

Notes

1

2

3

4

5

6

7

8

9

10

Notes

11

12

13

14

15

16

17

18

19

20

STUDY QUESTIONS

1. Verse 1: What are some reasons we should praise the Lord?

2. Verses 2–5: How do these verses show both the majesty and the mercy of the Lord?

3. Verses 8–9: How is God involved in His creation?

4. Verse 11: In whom is the Lord pleased?

5. Verses 15–18: What does God control by His word? What does the psalmist mean by "word" here (Ps. 33:6; Heb. 1:3)?

6. Verses 19–20: What great privilege did God give Israel among the nations? What does the psalmist mean by "word" here (Ps. 119:16)?

DEVOTIONAL REFLECTIONS

1. If the Lord has blessed us, praise is the most suitable response; and the more blessed we feel, the more our hearts will well up with gratitude and the more we will want to express greater praise. The Lord is looking after the whole world and since His people are more precious to Him than everything else, we can be assured that He will take special care of us. Since His compassions are new every morning, what do you need to stop worrying about, and for what should you start trusting God?

2. The greatest gift from God is His Word. Even today many millions of peoples do not have access to the Scriptures in a language they can understand. Yet how precious is His Word. It is powerful, for it is the Word of He who rules all things. It is full of wisdom, for it is the Word of He who is infinite in understanding. It is a message of hope and salvation, for it is the Word of the compassionate and merciful God. If you have a Bible that you can read in your own language, then thank God for it, read it daily, attend the worship service of a church where it is faithfully preached, and pray that God would use you to help others to receive this invaluable gift of God's Word.

Notes

1

2

3

4

5

6

7

8

9

10

11

12

13

14

STUDY QUESTIONS

1. Verses 1–4: What does the psalmist call on to praise the Lord?

2. Verse 5: Why should they praise the Lord?

3. Verse 8: What does the wind do?

4. Verses 11–13: What kinds of people should praise the Lord? Why?

DEVOTIONAL REFLECTIONS

1. All creation praises God and testifies to His glory, from the mightiest angel to the smallest bird. How much more should mankind, the apex of creation, praise Him! Even more so, His redeemed people ought to praise His name. Let us seek to excel in this most excellent work. Praise should be integral to both private and public worship. When in private prayer, begin with praise and not with a list of your needs and requests. In the worship of God's house, make a joyful noise. We should never be at a loss in the praise of His name. Are you eager to praise the Lord?

2. A fundamental belief of Christianity is the absolute distinction between the Creator and His creation. There are great differences among what God has created, whether angels, stars, sea monsters, mountains, cattle, kings, or infants. However, they all fall into one category: those which were made by God and therefore should praise Him (v. 5). Worship belongs to God alone, for "his name alone is excellent; his glory is above the earth and heaven" (v. 13). On the one hand, this should impress us with a humbling realization that we exist for His glory. On the other hand, it shows us that Christ our Savior is God, for He is to be worshiped (Heb. 1:6; Rev. 5:8–14). How are we tempted to worship part of God's creation rather than the Creator?

Notes

1

2

3

4

5

6

7

8

9

STUDY QUESTIONS

1. Verses 1–2: Where should Israel praise the Lord? With what attitude?

2. Verse 4: Why should God's people praise the Lord?

3. Verse 6: What should Israel have in their hand? How might we apply that today (Heb. 4:12)?

DEVOTIONAL REFLECTIONS

1. We find delight in people who already appear beautiful or honorable. It is a notable mark of God's grace that He delights to take the poor, humiliated, and ugly who trust in Him and make them lovely and glorious (Ps. 149:4). He is a King who does not take riches from His people, but joyfully gives to them. How does Christ beautify His people with the graces of justification, sanctification, and glorification? How should this motivate us to praise Him?

2. Zeal for God's praise motivates God's people to fight against all powers that oppose His kingdom (vv. 6–9). In the old covenant, this required physical violence to preserve the nation of Israel and bring God's judgments on the wicked (Pss. 18:34–44; 101:5, 8; 144:1). Since Christ abolished Israel's earthly theocracy (Matt. 21:43) and established a heavenly and spiritual kingdom (John 18:36–37), this zeal expresses itself not in physical force but in sacrificial efforts to bring the Word of God to all nations (2 Cor. 10:3–6; Eph. 6:10–18; Heb. 4:12), until Christ returns to destroy His enemies (Rev. 19:15–21). How does your praise of God translate into zealous action to spread His Word throughout the world? If you are not a preacher, how are you using your vocation for His glory and working with the church to fulfill the gospel mission?

1

2

3

4

5

6

STUDY QUESTIONS

1. Verse 2: What are two great reasons to praise the Lord?

2. Verse 6: Who should praise the Lord?

DEVOTIONAL REFLECTIONS

1. Song is an integral component of worship and should be offered to God with joy and reverence. The command that God be praised with an orchestra of instruments (vv. 3–5) reflects the old covenant economy of temple worship instituted by David, who appointed the Levites to serve as musicians (1 Chron. 15:16, 24). No such requirement is made in the new covenant, where God's sanctuary is not a building where a nation meets, but a people gathered in local congregations (1 Cor. 3:16; Eph. 2:21–22). The New Testament directs its instructions for worship at the hearts and voices of the people as they are moved by God's Spirit (Eph. 5:18–20). Just as the Levites played a variety of instruments in harmony, so God's people are diverse but worship in one Spirit through Christ (Eph. 2:18). How is your church like a spiritual orchestra, with each believer an instrument played by the Holy Spirit to praise the Father through the Son?

2. Our worship of God must revolve around His personal glory and amazing works (Ps. 150:2). This should shape the content of our songs, which should primarily focus upon the triune God and not our works or feelings. It should also direct the feeling with which we sing, for the glory of God should impress us with reverent fear and awe even as we rejoice in Him. There is no place for superficial lyrics, mindless repetition, or casual attitudes in the worship of God. Pray for a heart to praise Him and for such a filling of the Holy Spirit that this sacred work will be performed in a way that truly glorifies God.

3. It is fitting that the Psalter ends with a climactic call to praise God (v. 6). The Psalms take us through the full range of human experiences, but they center upon the glory of the Lord. They recount the history of God's people from creation through the second coming of Christ in a way that constantly reminds us that all God does in Christ He does to the praise of His glory (Eph. 1:6, 12, 14). This is God's ultimate purpose

for His creation. Have you embraced God's glory and praise as your ultimate purpose in life? If not, then your first act of worship must be to repent of your self-centeredness and idols, turn back to the living God, and trust in the Lord Jesus Christ to save you from your sins. If by grace God's glory has become your great aim, then devote yourself with all your might to living for His praise.